MW00654324

IMAGE, SENSE, INFINITIES, AND EVERYDAY LIFE

IMAGE, SENSE, INFINITIES, AND EVERYDAY LIFE

Michael Eigen

 **Routledge**
Taylor & Francis Group

LONDON AND NEW YORK

First published 2016 by
Karnac Books Ltd.

Published 2018 by Routledge
2 Park Square, Milton Park, Abingdon, Oxon OX14 4RN
711 Third Avenue, New York, NY 10017, USA

Routledge is an imprint of the Taylor & Francis Group, an informa business

Copyright © 2016 by Michael Eigen

The right of Michael Eigen to be identified as the author of this work has been asserted in accordance with §§ 77 and 78 of the Copyright Design and Patents Act 1988.

All rights reserved. No part of this book may be reprinted or reproduced or utilised in any form or by any electronic, mechanical, or other means, now known or hereafter invented, including photocopying and recording, or in any information storage or retrieval system, without permission in writing from the publishers.

Notice:
Product or corporate names may be trademarks or registered trademarks, and are used only for identification and explanation without intent to infringe.

British Library Cataloguing in Publication Data

A C.I.P. for this book is available from the British Library

ISBN-13: 9781782203728 (pbk)

Typeset by V Publishing Solutions Pvt Ltd., Chennai, India

CONTENTS

ABOUT THE AUTHOR

Michael Eigen is a psychologist and psychoanalyst. He is Associate Clinical Professor of Psychology in the Postdoctoral Program in Psychotherapy and Psychoanalysis at New York University, and a Senior Member of the National Psychological Association for Psycho-analysis. He is the author of a number of books, including *Toxic Nour-ishment*, *The Psychoanalytic Mystic*, *Feeling Matters* and *Flames from the Unconscious*.

PREFACE

This book spans a vast array of images, sensing, and portrayals of moments of my life as a psychotherapist and many excerpts from sessions. I have been fascinated by images ever since I can remember. How embarrassing for my mother, proudly introducing her three-year-old son to the principal of the school at which she taught only to have the little one say, "You're a whale." To this moment, I can see myself seeing this good man as a whale, as vividly as the instant it happened. As if his body and demeanour became a prompt for a waking dream image selected from swarms of inner possibilities, seas of images within. To see people as images evoked even more than their spatial presence. For the little boy, they *were* these images and, at times, this led to trouble.

Wilfred R. Bion wrote a good deal about "verbal images" and for a poet, verbal images can create experiential realities. I'm no longer sure when I became aware that words were packed with colour and tone. I could actually hear music and see colours when writing and sometimes speaking, as if words were colours and tones and the latter words. The separation ordinarily made between such media did not obtain for me. It appears that later in life I was spontaneously drawn to and profoundly influenced by psychoanalysts who painted, drew, and had a feel for poetry and music—Marion Milner, D. W. Winnicott, and Wilfred Bion.

I have written about the pervasive importance of sensing in earlier writings (2004b, 2014a). *Sense* is a word that spans many dimensions of experience, a kind of unifying word: e.g., the five or six senses, proprioception and kinaesthesia, common sense, animal or vital sensing, sense as meaning, intuition, a felt sense, a self-sense, a sense of self and other, God-sense. A lot of sensing goes on in psychoanalytic sessions, being with one's self and others, and in writing.

My major background is psychoanalysis but I have been in many forms of therapy, including Jungian, gestalt, and various forms of body work. I have gained from all of them. At the same time, therapy did not "cure" problems I wished addressed when I began as a young man but other, unexpected kinds of growth occurred. To my astonishment, problems I hoped therapy would address lifted in unanticipated ways as I aged, and continues at a more rapid pace as an old man (2014b, 2014c, as well as this work). So much in life is unexpected. When I entered analysis I never expected to become an analyst. It had never occurred to me. But little by little it became inescapable and soon I gave everything to it. I suspect it not only saved my life, but enabled me to enter a fuller existence.

Chapter One: "Being born", expresses birth processes that attend the life of a therapist and go on as long as life lasts. Bion felt that psychoanalysis is embryonic, not yet born or in uneven processes of birth. Throughout my life, I have heard people speak about appreciation of time one has left, especially if they know they are soon to die—the phrase, "making the most of each moment as if it were your last", comes to mind. In face of the ultimate I've tried the attitude of living each day as the last but it never worked for me. What works better for me is living each day, each moment as the first. That sounds something like Bion's encouragement to be without memory, desire, understanding or expectation in sessions, as if being with the patient for the first time, perhaps another reason why I gravitated towards him.

Spiritual images have been concerned with birth, different kinds of births, since ancient times. I use them as psychological twins with depth therapy concerns. There is good reason Freud remarked to Fliess that psychoanalysis is akin to ancient mysteries concerned with personal transformation. As I noted in *The Psychotic Core* (1986), Freud used imagery drawn from spiritual life to give expression to creative processes. We will see psychological-spiritual experience intertwine in this chapter and book.

Chapter Two: "Image from the bushes" begins with Alan, a person with a history of hospitalisations, saying, "Images are magical. Sometimes when I least expect it I see something that isn't there. After a moment I realise, it is there, behind my eyelids. I start to look at it and it changes. Another image comes. I can't catch them but I get glimpses. They come from the bushes. They disappear into the bushes."

The chapter traces the workings of various kinds of images, including "verbal images" and experiences they express and create. Images document, magnify, and amplify affect flow, which they may freeze or stimulate. Many dream images have to do with dreads and helplessness and break off as affect intensity mounts, aborting experiences they try to work with. Others portray strengths and capacities one undervalues or may not be aware of, growth possibilities or growth that already occurred or is in process of happening that one has not taken in. Images play a role in creating, distilling, and digesting experience.

It has taken a long time for images to be explicitly valued and given a significant role in the growth of experience and thought, as noted in the following quotation from Chapter Two:

> "Images have not always had a happy history in western epistemology, often seen as second class citizens along with sensation compared with thought. I tend to see various capacities as interpenetrating and informing each other. Sensation opens worlds of experience, adds colour to life. Images can function in rich, symbolic ways, encoding memory and touching future experiential dimensions. The poet, Thomas Traherne somewhere called perception a form of imagination, a thread Marion Milner (1987) develops. She values the life of images, how loaded they can be with opposite feelings and values, yet also stillness, null moments, creative void."

Throughout this chapter and book, discussion of the work of images and sensing intertwines with dialogue from sessions. Sometimes session dialogue or discussion go on without comment but they often are interwoven.

Chapter Three: "Fermenting devils in psychosis" continues my long exploration of devil images in madness and social life (one might say, madness, creativity, and destructiveness of social life; 1986, 1993, 2009,

2010, 2012), an exploration ongoing sixty years. The depth psychology work I've been most attracted to and immersed in gravitates towards work with psychotic dynamics. The devil has a long history in culture. Satan as biblical accuser or adversary has found internal counterparts in Fairbairn's or Bion's depictions of psyche working against itself, not only attacking but nulling, undoing, tearing apart its own existence, something Satan would be proud of. Bion goes farther by depicting a force that goes on working after everything has been destroyed, feeding on destruction itself. The traditional seductive aspect of the devil appears, psychoanalytically, in the psyche's attraction to, fascination with, attachment to and cathexis of demonic elements.

William Blake brought out creative and imaginative functions of the devil within, e.g., *The Marriage of Heaven and Hell*, presaging obsession with inner doubleness that marked a nineteenth century thread of creative literature, including the advent of Freud (Eigen, 1986, Chapter One).

As soon as the devil appears, cosmology appears and vice versa. What is the nature of the universe, our psychic universe, our world or worlds? Do we sense basic goodness or evil or something beyond these categories? Infinities of evil and good open infinities of experiential dimensions. Infinities are part of everyday life and the imaginative creation of life that creates us, an exploration still beginning.

Chapter Four: "Where is body?" was written on invitation by Asaf Rolef Ben-Shahar, Noa Oster and Liron Lipkies for their book, *Speaking of Bodies* (forthcoming, 2016). My assignment was to write on the "divine body", a subject with much appeal as I often have experienced the body as holy, divine, wondrous, a significant current among the spectrum of possibilities. I often think of Saint Paul's expressive outburst, not knowing where body or mind or *he* is when transported by grace. One might say seized by, infused by, and permeated by grace. Categories of hell, heaven, purgatory (in Buddhism the six realms of existence: Titans, hungry ghosts, hell, animal, heaven, human) are ancient poetic depictions of felt states of being. No one is exempt from pain and suffering and awful surprises and many also are "surprised by joy" (one of the defining characteristics of human existence; Eigen, 2001a).

In this chapter, I trace variations, the ins and outs, of body states that not only enriched but changed my life, as well as tracing important moments for patients. Body experiences are an inextricable part of spiritual systems (good heart, bad heart, organ sensation, emotion, spirit). One only has to think of Kabbalah's *sephirot* ("tree of life") or Hindu chakras to open fields of experience that include yet go beyond what we normally call body to the body ineffable. Bion speaks of infinities of emotional life, furthering dialogue between psychoanalysis and mystical dimensions of living (Eigen, 2012, 2014a).

Chapter Five: "There is no no" was written on invitation by Nelly Cappelli for *Psiche: Rivista di cultura psicoanalitica* (2014d, pp. 307–319). Its Italian title is: "Non c'è nessun no". Some forty years ago I wrote a paper on time and dreams (1983a), delineating time structures in dream life. A diversity of experience exists simultaneously and oscillating. If we take psychic structure as a whole, yes *and* no inhabit us, qualify each other, amplify and colour experience.

In this chapter, I playfully vary ways yes and no interact and see what we find in no worlds and yes worlds. No can have complex relations with itself depending on many factors. The chapter starts with Freud, Bruce (my patient), and I interweaving visions and thoughts. We are led through Biblical stories, Lacan, Tao, and Jodorowski's *El Topo*, sometimes a pirouette, sometimes a picador stirring up bulls, sometimes a butterfly chasing rainbows.

Chapter Six: "Shame" depicts what one might call shame with a thousand faces, or should I say "tooshies", since shame so often is associated with bottoms. Like Freud's libido, shame spreads through body and thought, liquid, electrical, congealing, fixating. It has been associated with holes, phalli, hearts and brains. A great hiding place for the sense of shame is the asshole but it spreads through body, surface, and depth, permeating one's sense of being. Aspects of self-image are tainted by shame. Its use in culture is myriad, from shaming a child to killing oneself. There are moments when the black hole of shame stimulates enlightenment, seemingly impossible but in keeping with our paradoxical sense of life. We may be ashamed of aliveness, ashamed of deadness—there is no end (pardon the language) to what shame may slip into and attach itself.

Shame can fuse with guilt and intensify self-hate. This chapter touches different relationships between shame and guilt but shame is centre stage (for portrayals of guilt in Wittgenstein, Levinas, and Bion, see *Emotional Storm*, 2005). Freud, Bion, bible stories, and Punch and Judy function as prompts, with Bateson and Bohm part of the brew. We pull on diverse threads of shame without quite knitting a whole. Complexity of our makeup is honoured. The main part of this chapter involves ongoing acts of expression by Peter, my patient, and my own thoughts, in response to Peter's, although it can be hard to tell who is responding to whom. I tend to keep much of what I am thinking to myself but our talk and thought unfold common concerns, overlapping in our ways. We may wish we developed as a life form without so much shame and sometimes feel stained by shame through and through, but monstrous acts committed shamelessly quicken appreciation of positive functions of shame in modulating mutuality.

Chapter Seven: "My session with André" was written on invitation by Edward Emery, who edited a special issue on French psychoanalysis for *The Psychoanalytic Review* (2015, volume 102), and is reprinted with the permission of the National Psychological Association of Psychoanalysis. Dr. Emery asked me to include my personal impressions. I trace my contact with Green from the first time I saw him in 1975 through some of our meetings during the next decades. He played a significant role in my personal and professional development. I taught his 1975 paper on changes in psychoanalysis for many years.

His analysis of a dream of mine in an analytic session played an important role in working through my resistance to marriage (which I sorely wanted). My sessions with Bion and Green within a year or two of each other, cleared the way for marriage and family that has lasted thirty-four years and still growing. Both he and James Grotstein, the subject of the next chapter, were among the first people I invited as speakers when I became Program Chair for the National Psychological Association for Psychoanalysis (NPAP). It is a pleasure to share some reminiscences and elaborate aspects of Green's contributions.

Chapter Eight: "Figments, facts, interruption, hints, and ..." is a chapter I was invited to write by Annie Reiner and Avedis Panajian for *Of Things Invisible to Mortal Sight: Celebrating the Work of James S. Grotstein* (forthcoming, 2016). Rather than simply writing about Grotstein's work, the editors suggested developing a chapter resonating with Grotstein's themes in my own way.

After starting with personal reminiscences, I take up themes from Grotstein's talks related to his writings, and weave tapestries with threads of Winnicott, Klein, Bion, Elkin, psalms, patients and, most of all, Bion's *A Memoir of the Future,* and the unfinished movie largely based on it. Some liken Bion's *Memoir* to Joyce or Beckett. Bion calls it "a fictitious account of psycho-analysis including an artificially constructed dream" (1991, p. 4). One could say, a dream of psychoanalysis. The movie was directed by Kumar Shahani and shot in India, where

Bion lived his first eight years. The script is by Shahani and Meg Harris Williams. Although the movie was never finished, it is packed with gems to mine. Near the end of the paper I add words from a character in a play of my own (2009) and touch an "indistinguishable" aspect of emotion and metaphor fading into and growing from the navel of dream.

Chapter Nine: "Changing forms" is made up of excerpts from sessions with a patient I call Tom. Moments probe existence in varying keys, especially crises of life and death, creativity, and destructiveness. Sessions gravitate to crises of faith. Is life worth living? Am I worth living it? With what quality? There is so much destruction in life and so much creativity. It is hard to reconcile with diverse aspects of our nature—and nature in general. We want to make it good and had God say about creation, it *is* good. We want to affirm basic goodness over evil. Tom and I, with each other and inside ourselves, dance with life and death, trying to find ways to affirm the human spirit and creativeness we so value. This chapter may seem fragmented but I find fragments an important part of existence, dense with wound, hope, desperation, peace, sometimes a life raft or a crowded search that itself becomes an opening.

Chapter Ten: "Some biographical notes" is a reworking of an interview Victoria Jean Dimidjian did with me over ten years ago for her book, *Journeying East: Conversations of Aging and Dying* (2004). Here I include my portion of the interview much elaborated, covering early life, college, trying to find myself as a young man, influences, and significant moments. Much has happened in ten years and continues happening. The interview with Dr. Dimidjian tended to emphasise my Buddhist inclinations, which I've tried to fill out with the importance of East and West in my life. Henry Elkin once remarked to me that if he wrote an autobiography he would call it *Neither East Nor West*. There is something in us grateful for rich influences yet unable or unwilling to be confined by them. We drink in and fight against at the same time. And moments go beyond anything we read or heard or thought about.

The Appendix has two book reviews I wrote on Marion Milner, separated by nearly thirty years. The first review was written in 1977, *On Not Being Able to Paint*. The second published in 2014, *Bothered by Alligators*. A concern that runs through her work is the creative spirit, particularly creativity and psychoanalysis, psychoanalytic creativity.

I feel Milner's appendix to *On Not Being Able to Paint* (1973) a classic in psychoanalysis, a condensed treasure of images related to creative processes. I taught it many years and each time got more from it. She wrote *Bothered by Alligators* (2012) towards the end of her life and was still working on it the day that she died at the age of ninety-eight. Permission for inclusion was given by the National Psychological Association for Psychoanalysis.

Milner writes openly about her depression during her son's child-hood, which she sees in his drawings, and includes a critique of Winnicott as her analyst. I wrote what might be the first critical appreciation of her work (1983b). She has been a living presence for me since the 1970s. Her focus on her own creative processes enhances appreciation of one's own creative sense, a gift that life does not stop giving. I thought bringing these two reviews together, separated by so many years, might evoke a feel for a profound continuity running through fragments of one's life.

CHAPTER ONE

Being born

Is psychoanalysis in process of being born? Is it in gestation? Gestation and birth together? Bion speaks of psychoanalysis as embryonic, sometimes a baby, and wonders what it may become. He speaks of the embryonic aspects of personality. But at times goes further, emphasising the relationship with what is not conceived, our relationship to the unknown. There is an unknown quality to an embryo, a penumbra of birth, movement ahead, and a rich feeling of possible happening. To meditate on what is unknown, not conceived, yet developing, a future coming towards us, an Ein Sof of the psyche.

In Jewish mysticism (Eigen, 2012), Ein Sof represents the unknowable infinite mystery beyond duality, existence, time, and space. A boundless infinite that, I feel, is part of human personality, at least in intimations. The God of creation, Yahweh, emanates from divine mystery, emanations that give birth to experience. I suspect when we try to describe such sensations, we touch what Winnicott (1992) calls an "incommunicado core" linked with Ein Sof within.

It is not far-fetched to link Kabbalistic portrayals of the birth of experience with psychoanalysis. Bion once told me, "I use the Kabbalah as a framework for psychoanalysis." If one looks deeply, one finds

1

convergence as well as difference. Here is a bit of applied "Kabbalah" in Bion's (1994, p. 214) approach to analytic sessions:

> "I am concerned in a session with what I do not know. The session is the only time when I can have contact with what I do not know; at any other time I can only have contact with, or think about, phenomena which I believe—rightly or wrongly—that I have already observed. But in the session I can have contact with phenomena that I have not so far observed, or have observed only partially. It is an opportunity that is not to be missed, for if it is it can never be repeated."

He goes on to write of the core of a session and core of a dream as an emotional experience seeking the best descriptions we can find, often given to us in seemingly unrelated fragments that a "selected fact" brings together in significant ways.

We may have convictions about what this emotional experience is. Sometimes, some of us are sure of what it is. It may be experienced fully, intensely or in hints, whispers, echoes. A meaning making processes attaches significance to it and that significance can change, grow, dissipate, look differently in different contexts, modified by further experience. An experience or significance can change size, seem big at one time, small another. It may take on different shapes, colours, tones, and spirits. An emotional sense threads through life, assuming different values.

In the quotation above, Bion gives special value to a session. Each session is a once in a lifetime happening, although we will have other once in a lifetime chances. Bion emphasises linking up with the unknown of the session, the emotional "ein sof" of the moment. A special opportunity for discovery, creative participation, healing, and growing. William Blake (Eigen, 1993) writes of creativity happening in the pulsation of an artery, special moments. For Bion, the session itself is a special moment. I don't think one would be mistaken to attach something of sacral significance to the chance it gives us.

Sensitivity to the unknown, absorption in the unknown is partly cultivated by dreaming: "I believe that the analyst may have to cultivate a capacity for dreaming while awake, and this capacity must somehow be reconcilable with what we ordinarily conceive of as an ability for logical thought of the mathematical kind" (1994, p. 215).

Dream-work in sessions and in poetry, art, logic. In *Cogitations* Bion drew what I call O-grams, a diagram or idea-o-gram showing culture (including art, science, religion) growing out of an unknown O, an unknown ultimate reality. In psychoanalysis, unknown emotional reality (1994, pp. 323, 325; Eigen, 2012). For Bion the core of a dream is an emotional experience, which is also a core of creative-destructive culture (Eigen, 2001a, 2002). In his last extended written work, *A Memoir of the Future* (1991), Bion gave expression to psychoanalysis as a dream, the dream of psychoanalysis.

Kumar Shahani (1983) directed a movie drawn from Bion's autobiographical works and *A Memoir of the Future*, but the movie was never completed. What we have are fragments with their own power and integrity. Kumar Shahani and Meg Harris Williams wrote the script, which may soon be published. You will find more information on the making of the movie in the notes that accompany it online.

A psychoanalytic dream, special value to each fragment—the analytic session which speaks through its cracks. An intimate caller—psyche speaking.

Not all births are welcome. In psychic reality there are monstrous births and rebirths as well as benevolent ones (Eigen, 1992). All manner of psychoanalytic babies. We are born all lifelong. Life as an extended moment, an extended birth and/or catastrophe. Bion speaks of a catastrophic impact of O that goes on and on, a kind of big bang of the psyche, bits and pieces flying away from each other and point of origin at accelerating velocity. What happens if a fragment lands on you or a patient? How can one know what it may be? The temptation is great to jump to conclusions or ignore it, but to let its impact work on you and keep on working is another matter. One fears being reborn as a monster or seeing the monster one is. But no one psychic moment is the one and only moment, even if at the time it seems so. Soon enough, other eternal moments qualify it. Alternate and varied infinities modulate one another, excessive as each may be when centre stage (Eigen, 1986). It is, in part, growth of faith that enables us to wait.

It was salutary to come upon a respected analyst who said the subject of analysis is unknown. Bion calls faith the psychoanalytic attitude. Faith, perhaps, in gestation and babies not yet born. Many mystics speak about the unborn and here we have it at the centre of daily sessions (Eigen, 2014c). It can be a scary business. Saint Paul: "What a dreadful thing to fall into the hands of the living God." One could also say how dreadful it may be falling into the hands of the living psyche. So many scary dreams portray psychic realities. A man told me how frightened he was of snakes in dreams as a child. He found dream snakes scarier than snakes in physical reality. The former terrified him. There seemed to be no escape from whatever dread they represented.

I knew from my own childhood how scary such dreams could be and many a night I turned on the light, looked under the bed and in the closet to be sure a horror was not there. A colleague of Bion's, Albert Mason, told Bion about a schizophrenic patient who kept turning on lights at night. Bion's supervisory response, "Everyone is entitled to a second opinion."

A second opinion came to me through many years of analysis and many more as an analyst. The need and possibility of a second opinion within grew over time with help. The need, value, and traction of a second opinion is often missing in psychosis and development of alternate inner opinions is crucial.

In time, my patient, too, developed further "opinions", views, and possibilities. As therapy accustomed him to more psychic contact, he came to see snakes as wisdom figures trying to convey a sense that there is more, that psyche is more than he had dreamed and that dreaming can grow too. Can we and our dreams grow together? Even death can mean different things at different times (Eigen, 1974). And a snake, including all its psychic snake powers, can take on different meanings in varied contexts (1981a).

Images sometimes used for the fear of God link with the fear of psyche. Seeing God and dying, for example, or the appearance of Krishna in the *Gita* as monstrous in human terms, or turning to stone facing Medusa, One might posit negative and positive infinities, much like Melanie Klein positing good and bad breasts (Eigen, 1996, 1998, 2007), and all the mixtures.

Here are several Bion quotes which refer to mystical experience but which he uses to depict aspects of psychic reality and growth of psychoanalysis:

> "The fundamental reality is 'infinity', the unknown, the situation for which there is no language—not even one borrowed by the artist or the religious—which gets anywhere near to describing it."
> (1994, p. 372)

"Many mystics have been able to describe a situation in which
there really is a power, a force that cannot be measured or weighted
or assessed by the mere human being with the mere human mind.
This seems to me to be a profound assumption which has hitherto
been almost completely ignored, and yet people talk about 'omnipotence' as if they knew what it meant and as if it had a simple con-
notation." (1994, p. 371)

What does investigation of the invisible and ineffable look like? With
what kind of tools? What is the sense that gives us such intimations?
Can it undergo development for the good of humankind?

Freud wrote that he would like to protect analysis from the doctors
and priests: "I should like to hand it over to a profession, which does
not yet exist, a profession of lay curers of the soul, who need not be doctors and should not be priests" (Freud, 1963, pp. 125–126).

Psychoanalysis—a profession that "does not yet exist". By "lay" he
means not medical doctors. Nor does he mean laying on of hands. One
thing he does mean is psyche to psyche, unconscious to unconscious,
a mysterious but very real contact with diverse impacts. Psychoanalysis
as a profession that does not yet exist, concerned with psychic work
coming into being, extended births over time (Eigen, 2014b). What kind
of births, with what quality? How long? How many stillbirths, monstrous births? What kinds of possibilities?

In a session with Bion in 1977, he told me to get married. Is this something that analysts are supposed to do? In this case, more than I can say,
I am so grateful. This was not something my own father didn't tell me
but from Bion it was believable. Why? How? Had I learned from early
childhood that my father usually wanted something from me for his
own ego? My marriage a feather in his cap? Yet when Bion said something similar, I felt free to begin to do it. As if reality itself spoke to me,
opened a gate. He spoke from a truth I could believe.

The first moment I saw him I felt, "I can tell him anything." The word
understand meant stand-under. This big man, taller than I by far, had
gotten under me, supported my psyche from below and I could breathe
and speak and listen, take in, wonder, think on and eventually do. He
made my life better, fuller, richer. Through various twists and turns,
four years later I married and became a father at the age of forty-five,
something I wanted to do and couldn't since my twenties. My life was
soon to grow faster and fuller than a foetus in the womb, the challenges

of getting along with wife, children, and profession. I would have to grow into a new existence if it was going to work.

In my early twenties I lucked out having a variety of work experiences in which I felt free to explore and experiment. At some point, I found myself working with disturbed children, including schizophrenic and autistic children, often with important contact with their families. In some cases, I was lucky to have very high quality supervisors, but even so, one was thrown on one's own resources moment to moment, sometimes sink or swim (better, sink *and* swim). This forced growth of capacity and, for me, such force was welcome. I was in love with creativity and the work squeezed more kinds of creativeness out of me than I knew about till then.

I knew from love relationships what a cauldron of pain and bliss contact with another person can be. I knew, too, from growing up in a family. But the idea of working with pain and its patterns and building capacity to tolerate and modulate distress in creative interaction with others and oneself was something different. I was learning from vicissitudes of therapy. Rather than simple helplessness in face of emotions, exercising them in a kind of psychic gymnasium had benefits. Not that helplessness is overcome but even one's helplessness can be a fount of meditation and stimulate rich moments one might have missed through pseudo control or dismissal. In my twenties I learned how rich working with madness can be and how, to the extent possible, staying with fields of experience brings rewards.

It wasn't until I was thirty that I began work on a one-to-one basis with adults. Two people alone in a therapy room in a clinic. I couldn't wait. From my first moments I felt like a fish in water. Here was air I could breathe, a psychic medium I could function in. Was I finding what I was made for?

I soon became aware of a hitch. Without quite realising, I was being my therapist and my patients at the beginning were me. A mania of sorts. It gradually dawned on me I thought all I had to do was act like my therapist and my patients would get better. But life did not let me get away with this. Actually, I had enough psychic contact to be helpful to most people I saw. But there came points in sessions, increasingly, that I felt I was losing out by not discovering how to be me and letting my patient be someone other than me. I was losing out on therapy life by unconsciously pretending to be who I wasn't and not registering fuller reality of the patient's own-ness.

Years of struggle ensued, little by little chipping away at my identification with my therapist, in so many ways helpful, but also a barrier to more real contact. When I saw Bion ten years later, at age forty, he still felt the need to encourage me "to begin the nasty business of being yourself". I thought I was moving along by then and he was telling me to begin. To begin and begin again and again. Now, more than thirty-five years later, approaching eighty, I often feel on the verge of beginning. An invitation that does not die. As if beginning becomes a place one enters, lives from, explores.

So at thirty I had to learn how to be a therapist who was not simply my therapist and be with people who were not simply me. Quite a challenge. New difficulties pressured new growth. This is one of the beautiful things about this hard work—and it *is* or can be more than hard. Impassables and impossibles become avenues of change. Blocks and trauma that had and perhaps have no answer, become ingredients in creative work, colour on the palette of living. Personalities—as the sephirot in Kabbalah or chakras in Kundalini yoga testify—are amazing, often with the emphasis on maze (Eigen, 2012, 2014a, 2014b).

Another overturning came in the wake of becoming a father at the age of forty-five. By then, I had been in the mental health world over twenty years and doing one-to-one and group therapy fifteen years. A new thing that began to happen was falling asleep in sessions, a habit that never entirely left. I learned about Freud falling asleep with his British but not American patients, the latter paying more and demanding more. I learned about others, like Winnicott, dosing—maybe to dose it out.

Contact dosage was something I already learned from clinic work. Some people can't take much contact, some can't take not having too much. Too much or too little. I suspect I am closer to needing too much *and* too little, depending on the swing of events and mood. Need for intensity on the one hand, need for fasting on the other, a kind of psychic bulimia, hunger for extremes. One is not always in the ballpark by trying to tie missing sessions with transference reactions, important as this is. There are people who miss sessions like they miss many things, as part of a way of life, running from danger of being overwhelmed. Lack of capacity to sustain contact. The problem, as Winnicott (1971) and Balint (1968) suggest, is not simply transference of a pattern but need to build capacity for experience.

I brought up my sleepiness to Phyllis Meadow (2003), a lively doer in psychoanalysis. She spoke about her own dosing off and related it to a baby part that felt trust. With some patients she wouldn't dare fall asleep. She'd be too anxious. They did not have the comforting tone that promoted letting go, like mother singing to baby. She said it was a compliment to the patient to be able to trust them with a dose. Dr. Meadow was not so naïve to think this the only possibility. She knew the usual rap about therapist sleep as a response to being threatened by the patient, and much else. It would be easy to call her or my tack a rationalisation but I think she designed her response in the moment, giving me a taste on the spot of maternal support.

It is also likely that my dosing off is a kind of contact dosage, not simply because of the patient, but because of my own challenged capacity to sustain contact. I think of babies falling asleep and waking many times throughout a day, not being able to take too much waking consciousness. A kind of dialectical swing of states of being. I heard D. T. Suzuki speak of his own intermittent dosing and waking in old age, like a baby, which he let be, riding waves of life.

Hyman Spotnitz (2004), Dr. Meadow's teacher, often spoke of regulating the amount and kind of contact a psychotic patient can take. He had formulas like staying away from subject oriented focus, since the individual could not take too much of this. Instead, he suggested asking three to five object oriented questions per session. This may sound simple and formulaic but it can be varied with subtle nuances in very healing ways. Over time, little by little, a person is able to sustain more complex, varied and colourful interactions, which would have flooded and made him/her withdraw or aggress earlier. I outline growth of complexity in recovery from psychosis in *Contact with the Depths* (2011, Chapter Seven, "Tears of pain and beauty"). While following my own bent, many "schools" and therapeutic styles have become a natural part of my work.

Then again, there may be more to my sleepiness than my contact deficiencies. A significant detail in my new situation involved staying up at night with a baby, moulding to a being with intermittent sleep. One of the pitfalls of parenthood not emphasised enough is fatigue. The fatigue of caring for another whose needs do not fit with adult work schedules. I have to marvel at Dr. Meadow's intuitive sense. She could have asked me, "Has something changed in your life? Are you taking care of a baby?" Instead, she slipped into the feel of the situation, parent and baby, and this spread to my patients.

As months and the first years of parenthood ticked by, I discovered I was becoming a different person with my patients, a different being. The sense of caring for a child, a breakthrough of love, so wanting good for a person, began leaking, transferring to those in my therapy care. Becoming a father, little by little made me more fatherly. I was still a spontaneous, irascible child. But something was added. Another dimension of care and love and support. I always tried my best, but this was something further, wanting to be the best possible therapist I could be, wanting to do well by another, as I would want to do well by my children. Dr. Meadow found me out before I knew myself.

By this time, I already was moving into more complex territory with Winnicott, Klein, Bion, Kohut. As I wrote in the introduction to *The Psychotic Core* (1986), many schools are part of me. I tend to see all therapists as one therapist with many faces and arms, like a multi-ocular-limbed Buddha. What someone can't get from me, one might from another. We all have something to offer, our own selves, our own ways. We contribute what we can to the general pool. But, the work is also individual, alone, deeply pressing. I do not like therapy wars as I've personally gotten so much from the way different people approach experience, as well as differences in areas of experience approached.

It was 1981—marriage, fatherhood. When I sat down to write I found myself writing about faith from a deeper, fuller, permeating faith. In 1986—my second child was born, my father died several months later, my major analyst died before the year ended, my first book came out. Tears and joy and love and depths. Life was beginning—again, still. Isn't this part of daily existence—life beginning? Deeper engagement with spirituality, work, family. Falls and rise of spirit, so many kinds of spirit. What does love do with us? A saving rape of the soul by love? How much life can we take? How much of ourselves?

What kind of love? Humanity has written about many kinds of love and perhaps even more nuances find expression in art and music. As is often the case, dichotomous thinking comes to the fore to over-organise experience. For example, the old binary agape-Eros, akin to spirit-matter. Divine and erotic love, selfish-unselfish love, self-love, other-love, as if the two can be separated. From Homer to Shakespeare we know about destructive sides of Eros, jealousy, envy, pride, ambition, greed, hate, murder (Eigen, 2001a, 2002). All manner of combinations: love saves, truth kills; truth saves, love kills.

Bion writes of narcissistic-socialistic elements of emotional life. He, too, draws a distinction between animal and divine love (1994, pp. 371–372). "A lioness nuzzles and shows every sign of feelings of love and affection—if interpreted in human terms—for prey it has destroyed; but it is murderous love, the love that destroys the loved object." Nourishing and destructive aspects of parental love can be fused (Eigen, 1999, 2001b). Often we take in emotional toxins in order to find emotional nourishment.

At the same time, sexual, murderous and parental love can defend against perception of psychic life as such, particularly as it mediates "the terrifying unknown which cannot be described in physical, sensuous terms—or if it is, it is much more likely to mislead than to illuminate" (Bion, 1994, p. 371). In such a context, Bion suspects a term like "love of God […] at least makes an attempt to introduce an element that shows that it is not a discussion about something that is so simple as physical love known to the human animal" (1994, p. 372). In a related way, Tausk's "influencing machine" (Eigen, 1986) is not simply related to body fears but invasion and take-over of mind and psychical being by invisible, indefinable, boundless mind or spirit. The "unknown" for Bion is a kind of ontological and trans-ontological reality.

Truth alone cannot get us out of this: (1) because it is limited; and (2) our use of and approach to truth is complex and varied. So much use of truth is cruel, selfish. I learned from early childhood that one uses "truth" to get one's way, to dominate. In *Coming Through the Whirlwind* (1992) I studied a man who used therapeutic truth to almost destroy his life. As Bion (1994) points out, there is cruel and compassionate use of truth, approaches to truth, relationships with truth. Our use and approach to our capacities is framed by affective attitudes. We are always in complex relationships with what we talk about and how.

Then there is death. All the small deaths we undergo and some great deaths. And simply death itself, the fact, the reality. When I was a young man I was very frightened of death. There were periods I courted suicide, stuck my head in an oven, walked blindly into traffic, crossed a river walking on the outer side of bridges (having climbed over the safety bar), and God knows what prevented me getting killed on my motorcycle, the chances I took—all and more a kind of counter-phobic Russian roulette. I am grateful for failure. I have been helped by failure many times in my life, as if failure were a protective angel trying to save me from myself.

Part of the unknown: moments you would not expect happening in ways you could not have guessed that have immediate transforming impact—just like that, out of the blue. As if the unknown taps you and says—check this out, this is big. You don't have a leg to stand on because it happened out of the depths, nameless grace or terror. One such moment happened to me when I was thirty-one, visiting my dying aunt, one of my mother's sisters, in the hospital. In a few moments, my fear of death diminished. I won't say was gone, done with. That's too much, although it seemed that way for some time. A decisive corner was turned and, in instants, the old death anxiety and suicidal threats in face of it were gone.

You can find more details about this and other biographical happenings in *Conversations with Michael Eigen* (Eigen & Govrin, 2007). Here let me tell an important part of it. My Aunt was bitter that she was dying. "Mike, I didn't expect it so soon", she said. She had worked so hard and this was her reward. I held her hand quietly, which seemed to comfort her a little, and as we looked at each other in silence I could not tell where life left off and death began. The room became peaceful, her eyes closed. It was our last time together. The tranquil moment grew and when I left I realised my fear of death dissolved. I tested this for many years but now it simply is part of my being.

This was not anything I expected but such happenings build respect for psychic possibility. I discovered, over time, new feelings with patients who had similar dreads, sometimes disabling. I did not have answers, but was aware the as yet unknown could come about, without knowing when or how. I learned to keep situations open even in the depths of despair. And when it seemed most respectful to simply accept impossibility of help, the tone and texture of acceptance had resonance not known before.

I have thought many years about the Zen saying, be a corpse, and I've heard that the Dalai Lama meditates on death three hours a day. The reality of death is emphasised in religions, whatever they may say about it. Perhaps there is a way we do not think we will die and a way in which we think we will. Freud's dictum that there is no death in the unconscious in conjunction with his postulating a death wish, suggests the multi-dimensional complexity of our sense of reality and the importance unreality plays in our lives (a word close to lies).

For many years I seemed to translate religious language to psychological experience. Feeling more alive or dead as moods, affect states. We feel life arising or dying out at varied times, daily or over longer periods. Different kinds of aliveness and deadness (Eigen, 1996). This is not the whole story, of course. But something would be lost if we did not see the emotional dramas religious narratives portray (Eigen, 2002, 2011, 2012). Tao sometimes speaks about there being only life. One can feel this at times and reach this state through meditation. But there are other currents Bion refers to as the multi-coloured dome of glass that stains the white radiance of eternity, an image culled from the poet, Shelley. The many emotional colours of life, each opening worlds. The multi-coloured life of therapy, each with worlds to open, disclose, create.

Fast-forward to my current age, approaching eighty. Will I reach it? My father died months before his eightieth birthday. My major analyst died in his early seventies, which I've passed. Winnicott and Guntrip at seventy-five, which I've passed. Freud and Bion at eighty-two. My eye catches the arc of time of artists in a museum visit. Analysts who reached one hundred? That won't be me. I've worn myself out with experiencing. But when?

In my seventies I have already experienced two illnesses that could kill me. I have a reprieve, a caesura, and appreciate that I had serious warning and was not snatched instantaneously, as happened to some I knew. I have time to undergo transformations that death's immanence evokes. I have time to say good-by to myself. I can't say I always make best use of the gift of time, but much has happened I am grateful for, events that refused me until now.

When I entered serious analysis for the first time at age twenty-one, my presenting complaint was something rotten, wrong, off, an infection inside. I was hoping therapy would alleviate it, make it go away, fix it. Other things happened but not that. The ill feeling persevered, at times fading in the background, barely perceptible, playing less of a role in the field of experience. New experiences grew. Life grew. But it was not until my seventies that the presenting complaint fully lifted. It happened in an instant, again unpredictably, a moment out of the blue, just like that. One moment it was there, the next gone. What relief, fresh breath. I still feel the ease in my chest that suddenly appeared.

I have written about this in various places (e.g., 2014b, 2014c). It happened upon reading about the *yechida* soul in a book by Rabbi

Menachem Schneerson (1998). Kabbalah/Chassidus posits a number of souls (somewhat akin to yoga positing chakras, energy centres). I suspect Aristotle's varied souls plays a background role in this (Eigen, 2012). In Jewish mysticism soul dimensions include a vital soul, higher and lower emotional souls, intellectual soul, intuitive soul, and a soul essence in immediate contact with God's essence. This latter is called the yechida soul, one with God.

When I read about the soul's essence in immediate, enduring contact with God's essence, the bad feeling that touched me in the background of my being (often in the foreground earlier), dissolved. I had read the same book ten years earlier and found it worthwhile and enriching but not essentially transformative. In my seventies the cessation of the rotten or bad or infection feeling happened in a moment, almost as fast as I read the words in Schneerson's text, instantaneously. Touching the yechida soul changed my experiential world and since then, has helped me with clients (Eigen, 2014c, for example). How did that happen? Why? Where did this experience come from?

Another transformative moment in my late seventies happened in relation to not being able to forgive myself. It is easier for me to forgive others than myself. There are things that I have done that are unforgivable. No matter how I approached them, years of analysis, prayer, meditation, nothing budged. I probably reached the conclusion that I was stuck with not forgiving myself, as I had felt stuck with the ill feeling that surprisingly gave way late in life. Then one day, in an instant, without warning, I found myself in Jesus. I would say imaging Jesus. Thoughts of being forgiven were buzzing, forgiven through Jesus. It seems more than imaging. Impalpable, indefinable. Without being able to say how, it was as if Jesus touched the unforgiving spot and it was healed. An ineffable instant and the hard rock, the unyielding, unforgiving place ebbed. Again new space, freshness, breath.

These are two great events in my latish seventies concerning inner knots that were unyielding. A practical effect in my work is continued growth of respect for and sensitivity to unknown processes. One can think of many ways to understand this. A factor for me seems to have to do with the press of death opening possibilities of experience, a fuller sense, less contracted, less congealed. Who knows what the next moment will bring? The unknown as seedbed of possibility as well as catastrophe. How simple it sounds and what a difference it makes. And at the moment, there is still time.

Nina Coltart (1993, 1996) links the heart of therapy with mystery. We had sparse contact with each other but had some awareness of each other's existence. She (1995) reviewed a book of mine and liked it and I was aware of simpatico vibes. Then one day a voice on the other end of the telephone says she's Nina Coltart, passing through New York City on the way to speak at Austen Riggs. She asked herself, what did she want to do in New York City? The answer: "Say hello to Michael Eigen." And so we did. I mumbled something about travelling by herself and she responded that she likes to go places alone. I got the sense of having a good built in travel companion. How to make friends with oneself—no easy business. I felt a glow when she hung up and hope she did too. Two alone people appreciating each other's presence.

I learned that we also share a book together. Interviews Anthony Molino did with each of us separately are in his book (1998). How shocked he was when he called Nina for a further, scheduled talk and learned that she committed suicide. I think of great analysts who killed themselves, among them Freud, Karen Horney, Nina, in the face of the irreversible deterioration of illness. Can I know if this will be my fate? It is profoundly touching how we can be touched by even a moment's contact of someone passing through, as happened with Nina and I. As Bion once told me, "We must seize these moments when we can." But in fact, I suspect, they seize us, touch us with flowing impacts.

I sometimes wonder if my earlier or later patients were better off. Who had the better therapist? At one point in my life I began to think, I wish I could work with some of my early patients now. I'm sure I could do better. About that time, I received a call from one of my first patients out of the blue. She looked up my number and called, saying she thought it might be good for me to know how much I helped her. We had worked together forty years earlier. She valued my encouragement to find and be her real self. She had done well, raised a family, her marriage was better than ever, and she enjoyed a good career in something she loved and was getting ready to retire. She told me her name and wondered if I remembered but the truth was I recognised her voice immediately. It was a call I valued and needed without knowing it. So my early self had its virtues. I'd better get a balanced view on all this and take in the good and bad of early and late, neither the answer, both contributors. Perhaps they can be introduced to each other, appreciate what each offers and prepare for still more unknown intimate visitors.

CHAPTER TWO

Image from the bushes

"Words create feelings. A poet creates feelings with words, makes new feelings when talking in the present. When you're speaking, when you're really speaking, you create feelings. Sometimes it's seamless. Words create feelings, feelings create words. The process includes and goes beyond both. It may be a deeper synchrony in our beings leads to both feelings and words, word feelings, feeling words" (Eigen, 2011a, p. 42).

"Words are images, images are feelings, feelings are …" quoted from a patient.

Images are magical. Where do they come from? One patient, Alan, said, "Sometimes when I least expect it I see something that isn't there. After a moment I realise, it is there, behind my eyelids. I start to look at it and it changes. Another image comes. I can't catch them but I get glimpses. They come from the bushes. They disappear into the bushes."

This is progress. Alan had been hospitalised for seeing things that weren't there. However, they did not simply appear and disappear, at least not quickly. They stayed a long time, changing the character of peoples' faces, making them seem monstrous, deformed, evil.

I did not minimise the possibility that he might be seeing evil that was there. Most of the time, we try to minimise our sense of evil in order to survive, function and feel better. To stay with it in a fruitful way takes a lot of courage and capacity. Most of us can't do it but perhaps dip in and out fleetingly. We can't really take too much of ourselves—one reason we feel we want and need more of ourselves, more realness.

In conversation the other day, someone said, "I hide from life to avoid death." She recalled a song from childhood, "Sinnerman." Sinnerman runs to the rock, says, "Please hide me." The rock says, "I can't hide you." Sinnerman runs to the river but it's bleeding, runs to the sea but it's boiling, runs to the Lord who says, "Go to the devil." The devil was waiting and Sinnerman cries with all his being, "Lord I need you. Don't you see I need you? You have the Power I need."

We hide within ourselves. Sometimes images bubble and show us hints of things we hide. How let them in, work with them? How pay attention a little more? How befriend and dwell with images that scare the hell out of us?

In a way, "Sinnerman" reminds me of "One little goat", the last song usually sung at the Passover Seder. The cat eats the goat, the dog bites the cat, stick beats the dog, fire burns the stick, water puts out the fire, ox drinks the water, the slaughterer kills the ox, the angel of death kills the slaughterer, and the holy one, blessed be he, smites the angel of death.

Here we have the stuff of dream images, so often concerned with dreads. Songs are often waking dreams. At the heart of dreams are feelings (Bion, 1994). Feelings here of a kind of ultimate helplessness. No earthly power can help us, not fully. We cry our hearts out to God. Is God, too, an image, an imageless image?

Beier (2006) details violent God images we use and argues that we have created false gods with our violent images, expressive of our violence. For him God is love. It is a beautiful portrayal. One could argue, aren't we loving too? Melanie Klein (1946; Eigen, 1996, 2007) outlines two central emotional nuclei, love and hate. Is it surprising our god images combine, split or otherwise express and demonstrate our emotional cores? It seems to take thousands of years to relocate feelings out there to in here.

No easy matter to turn the balance from hate to love, violence to peace. We are not sure how to do that or what that would mean. We have myths of transformation, sublimation and largely relied on narratives of control and struggle. Rumi's poetry often suggests making room for states and tendencies, welcoming all the guests within. We are still trying to learn how to do this, infants in face of such a challenge.

Alan went through much pain in attempting to change a little of the negative to positive. During an intermediate phase, he began to acknowledge that while the monsters he saw may be real, they were not the whole story. Most people he met were not simply or only monsters. Some people inspired him. And many he found nourishing and enriching in some way. It was appalling they could be wiped out in an instant by negative vision—turned into monsters in a flash.

Little by little, he began to see there was a magnification and narrowing process that blew up the worst in others and downplayed mitigating factors and goodness. Our work in therapy was a hub of this shift. Bad as I am, he could not see me as only bad. He sensed he was being helped by our being together, even if we didn't know how or how much. Our meetings took the edge off some of the horror and dread and, at times, with increasing frequency, he found he left sessions feeling better.

Alan never again needed hospitalisation and in less than a year took himself off medication. Several years later he tried to describe what happened. "A feeling of you stayed with me. I saw images of your face but often you were with me in an imageless way. If I had to locate the feeling, somewhere in my chest, a little higher, a little lower. Then it shifted, hard to pin down, a switch. My own presence began taking your place. The presence I felt was more me than you and I began to hear my own voice. It's a miracle when you hear your own voice, your tone, a sound that spreads through you.

"So many people speak in a tone that is not their own. Often I heard myself and wondered, who was that, as if my tone was to the left or right of me, not coming from my heart or gut or soul. I hear that in others, a tone too strident or mushy, as if the place speech comes from misses the person."

An image that vanishes in the depths and turns into tone, reversing from other to self. Images have emotional centres and, in this case, an emotional centre that tone distils.

Herbert Read (1955) wrote that image precedes idea by about two hundred years. Does some analogous sequence occur in individuals? Image as mediators of feeling on the way to thought? Experience teaches me that one can't count on a set rule when it comes to intermingling of sensation-perception-feeling-image-thought. Capacities are multi-directional and all kinds of patterns and mixtures occur.

One day, as time increased between Alan's last and final hospital stay and the new life he led, he spoke of a dream in which he was cheek to cheek with a young woman he had never seen and did not know. She was nice enough but not startling or crazy-making. A nice feeling. But also more than nice. The sensation he felt when their cheeks touched was nothing like he ever experienced. One might come close by calling it a touch of the sublime. Ineffable.

Not that it wasn't sexual but sexuality was not its main part. He wept thinking of it and felt chills up and down his back. Warm chills. It was one of the best feelings he ever had. In the dream they touched cheeks a number of times, sometimes let their cheeks touch longer. Now that he was awake, he tried to recreate the sensation, imagining the girl's cheek and his touching again. And again. To a certain extent, he could create the feeling he loved by imagining their dream cheeks touching. Not as complete and startling as in the dream, but a satisfactory hint, a feel that did not go away. Eventually it began to fade, remaining as a kind of reference point for what feeling can be, what life can feel like. What a gift his dream gave his waking life.

The residue of the felt sense remained after the image faded, as if the image carried the feeling and was less needed once the feeling became part of a feeling stream. Nevertheless, Alan found himself, from time to time, arousing the cheek to cheek image with its indefinable thrill. It more than calmed and reassured him. It raised the level of faith and affirmation. He began to wonder if love could be part of it and grow.

Images have not always had a happy history in western epistemology, often seen as second class citizens along with sensation compared with thought. I tend to see various capacities as interpenetrating and informing each other. Sensation opens worlds of experience, adds colour to life. Images can function in rich, symbolic ways, encoding memory and touching future experiential dimensions. The poet, Thomas Traherne somewhere called perception a form of imagination, a thread Marion Milner (1957, 1987) develops. She values the life of images, how loaded they can be with opposite feelings and values, yet also stillness, null moments, creative void. Earlier, I wrote of God as an imageless image. There is a Hindu saying that ordinary daily life is the past, dreams the present, and void the future. An intertwining of image and void with time—note Bion's book title, *A Memoir of the Future* (1991).

It seems to me that we are likely speaking of interlocking states that enter varied relationships with one another. Sound and silence, image and void. You need both for either to be possible.

The Biblical God warns against imagining and representing him. Chuang Tzu (1964) speaks of a true master with identity but no form. Bion (1994) writes that he cannot represent the experience of analysis but can evoke it. God gets mad when we worship "graven images". He speaks and the world comes into being from nothing. Mystics say God creates the world from nothing each moment: you are being created this moment out of nothing. There is a language of zero, nullification, a value of processes that cannot be imagined or conceptualised or represented. Are all the words in this paragraph creating an image? Is an underlying image sense creating these words? An imageless image?

Is there an underlying blank image at once both empty and full, an "image" corresponding to sensations the baby has on feeding? Or an overlapping dimension, the rise and fall of emotion, now filled, now empty of feeling? A sense that, in part, helps give birth to experience.

Even explicit images can be fuzzy. One wonders just what was in a dream that seems so clear, e.g., cheek to cheek. Instead of postulating war between zero and multiplicity, let's treat each as aspects of creativity, partners. Now there is nothing, now an image, a feeling, a word, a form, a thought—immaterial materials in the weave of life. We have a history of devaluing one or idealising another. What about acknowledging the riches each adds and partner their interplay. One moment nothing, next moment cheek to cheek, a new feeling. It begins to disappear but leaves a trace to grow with.

The feeling-image, cheek to cheek, seemed to come out of nowhere and began to return to nowhere. By lucky chance the dreamer awoke in time to feel a feeling their touch was part of. How to describe this? There are many ways. One is to posit an imageless image and underlying image sense—part of a vocabulary that tries to touch ineffable moments images sometimes help mediate. Images as psyche knocking on our door in hope that we will link with ourselves more richly. Images as helpers seeking to mediate rich contact between regions of being. Images as mediating links between sensation, feeling, thought and no-thing (akin to Keats's "spirit ditties of no tone", or Whitman's "wild trumpeter", now whirling like a tempest, now vanishing and coming again).

Alan says, "I fall through holes in my being." Unlike Korach (see below), he lives to tell about it. Or perhaps Korach is precisely an emblem of the holes beneath us, the holes within. Whatever holes he falls through, more appear. Verbal images. Instead of a literal hole, psychic ones. Psychoanalysis is a kind of expressive language, verbal images expressing feeling, a branch of poetics. Perhaps there comes a point where links and what is linked become indistinguishable.

A kind of holy cheese model. Does the cheese link the holes or holes link the cheese? One goes through life not only expecting to fall off the edge of the universe, but reaching a point where falling through holes becomes normative, a kind of home base, or one of our affective home modules. In this regard, Bion writes of a sense of catastrophe linking personality together.

There is a moment in the Bible when a group of Hebrews led by Korach (Numbers 16:1–18:32) challenge Moses's authority. "What gives you special right to tell us what to do? Aren't we all God's children? Why do you put yourself over us?" Some see this as a voice of democracy. Some see it as a political ploy of selfish ambition. It gets uglier and, finally, the two sides agree to make offerings and see whether God prefers Korach's or Aaron's (the high priest, Moses's brother). As it turns out, God preferred Aaron's and, to dramatise the matter, a hole opens up under Korach and his followers and the earth swallows them.

I once wrote a poem developing out of states melded in this story:

> You never know when you
> like Rumpelstiltskin
> will fall through a
> hole of your making
> an infinity beneath you
> just when you thought
> you could walk.
>
> dangerous to think you are
> better than Moshe
> but gosh
> does one ever
> stop falling through
> holes one walks on

does one make
another hole
with each step

are all steps mis-steps?
Did Korach fall forever
so Moshe could ascend?

Do they meet?
are they meeting now
backstage
while we view a performance
we take for real

is separation the hole?
the real?

where would we be
without the
opening

disappearing with
each movement of thought

Korach's idea
of freedom from the law
sedition against the state
of dream.

I am not proposing this as a good poem, but use it to point to verbal images and states of feeling. A sense of the ground opening under you. You never know when. Where do these holes come from? Our own emotional states that we lack resources for? Trauma impacts? Rigid attitudes? Are hole and infinity both verbal images? Does the verbal image slide or rely on implicit visual images, concepts, perceptions? As emphasised above, categories of experience are often opposed to one another but one senses inter-feed, fluidity, blends, parts of a pool of being.

Freud's (1925a) paper on the mystic writing pad touches this. You write something on the pad, pull the top sheet and what you wrote is gone. Or is it? Underneath the sheet you see traces of what you have written. Freud's discussion of memory and perception is helpful insofar as one does not have to decide which comes first or which is primary. They arise and work together, each contributing, functions of a living organism.

In the poem, too, we get a glimpse of the meeting and dissociation of opposites or different aspects of personality, different tendencies, Moshe (Moses) and Korach (e.g., law and dissent). What seems dissociated on one level, may meet and mutually contribute on another.

Again, a reference to opening-disappearing. Thoughts and feelings come and go, dream images appear and disappear. A sense of self may appear and disappear, as may a sense of God. Where is a dream that has disappeared? I've had experience of images I thought gone return unexpectedly and with them states that contribute to how life feels. Games rotating around here-gone, now you see it-now you don't begin in childhood and echo important characteristics of experience and function.

Moses dreams the law, Korach rebellion. Yet awhile earlier, Moses was a rebel in the land of Egypt. Freud posits the operation of reversal as earlier than repression. He was fascinated by mixed, oscillating, fluid, and rigid features of psyche. He even suggested that shifts in states between sleeping and waking (e.g., psychotic-like operations in dreams *vs.* more critical consciousness when awake) might harbour possibility for reversals that, someday, could enable effective work with psychosis. Isn't it, after all, the same psyche that produces Moses and Korach, at once dreaming law and rebellion into existence? Affect links remain fairly constant throughout history but the subjects and objects change (e.g., love and hate links endure but who loves or hates who changes).

Alan fell through holes in his psyche and life yet sat in a room and talked about them. Even after hospital (he had been hospitalised several times before this last one), he managed to get to my office. He never missed a session. The world was at once stable and buzzing for him. The phrase, "blooming, buzzing confusion" or Freud's "cauldron of seething excitations" refers here to emotional states, emotional storminess, buzzing, confusion, excitation, deadening, and many more. In Alan's case, the buzz and breakage had somatic aspects, psychical states affecting body, as well as the reverse.

Here he speaks of his drive to my office: "I wonder, will I make it? There is breakage in the sky, whirring in my brain. Suddenly, the sky streams into rivers, rips. When it's gentle, ripples. Have you ever seen the sky tear to pieces? As soon as I say that tear [rip] turns into tears [weeping]. They are the same thing but not the same. Does it scare you to think I am driving in a sky that is ripping open and falling and streaming? I hold on to the steering wheel. I grip it. The car shakes but is stable. The road quivers but is stable. A road is a road. I get here."

Over and over he tells me how much colours of the sky mean to him. Colour permeates, lifts, opens. Colour and expanse give him hope. They link earth and existence with infinity. Colour is like visual music and music, we say, is filled with colour. Auditory imagery. The ancients spoke of music of the spheres. Kant spoke of music of the moral universe. Keats wrote of inner music and "spirit ditties of no tone", evoked by images on a Grecian urn. The interplay of capacities, crossovers, and tendrils from a common pool. Interplay of madness and something beyond or other or not just mad.

There are so many accounts and tales of the lifting of barriers. Buddha sitting with suffering until it shifts to nirvana. Intense concentration on a point of experience opens the field of experience. In Freud's terms, a reversal, although in Buddha's case one might argue that something new is produced, another mode of experiencing and way of approaching experience. One could say something similar about Jesus on the cross, death and resurrection. An opening through agony, through horror and desolation. Again a reversal and opening, images at once visual and verbal.

A favourite of mine is Bodhidharma meditating in front of a wall for nine years (Eigen, 2011b). My sense of this has to do with greater and lesser walls within and how, from time to time, they lift or shift. Perhaps my very favourite is the story of Job, who loses everything and, ultimately, finds the great mystery (Eigen, 1995, 2011b, 2012). He is a magnifying lens through which to "see", intuit, feel, and study processes of contraction-expansion.

A discovery for myself through life has been that in the closed depths, there is something infinitely open. Not just the image of one door opening when another closes, although that's fine. But something more, deeper, less understandable. In the very depths of the unpacked density of the closed, in the depths of its very obdurateness and inaccessibility, there is an open infinity. When first finding this, it felt miraculous, mysterious. It may well be. But it has become something else for me with the years, part of my everyday working life, partly where I live.

Variations of this have been found by many of my patients. For example, Alan: "Things inside me I thought I'd never get rid of or would never budge have shifted. There's more give. Not that I'm not stuck. I'm plenty stuck. But not as stuck all the time. It's like, I go into a closed part, hit myself hard on closed parts, hit some more. Maybe a little like hitting big boxing bag that doesn't give way but you get stronger hitting it. Only inside some things do give way and you feel it. You feel the difference and I think, wow, how did that happen? Something really happened!"

I get from Alan that there are ways one *can* get stronger banging one's head against a wall. And sometimes the wall gives way to various degrees and something else happens. In my experience, going into density can connect with infinite openness.

Terms like packed, openness, dense are, partly, drawn from lived experience with the physical world. Jesus's burial cave was closed with a boulder and opened after three days. The image of open-close has been with us thousands of years. Eyes open and close. Nasal passages get blocked and open. Chest congested and clear, breath more fluid and stuck. Paths in valleys and mountains blocked or open. Mouth open or closed, lets in good things, keeps out, spits out bad. Open-closed, blocked-fluid are part of experience on many levels. Language for experience is multi-dimensional, packed with implicit (and often explicit) images spanning sensation, perception, intuition, words, and concepts. All capacities feed the image world and the latter feeds all capacities.

The Kabbalah speaks of "a spark of impenetrable darkness" flashing from depths of infinity, a spark that, akin to the big bang, ignites the universe into being (Matt, 1996). Rebbe Schneerson (1978) speaks of God creating the universe each moment from nothingness. *You* are in process of creation from nothingness each instant. Bion (1970; Eigen, 1998) writes of a catastrophic explosion at the origin of personality, a kind of big bang constituting personality and consciousness for good and/or ill, beginnings in which creativity and destructiveness are indistinguishable. Freud wrote of blinding himself artificially in order to focus light on one dark spot, a statement translated by Bion into a beam of intense darkness that brings out what illumination obscures (Grotstein, 2007).

Here again are seamless mixtures of visual and verbal images clustering around basic experiences: day-night, light-dark, perceptual elements that transform into a multiplicity of dimensions. So much so, these images become part of the language of mystical and creative experience, part of experience itself. Spiritual literature and poetry speak of the great light and creative darkness, pointing to experience that uplifts and transforms.

William Blake writes of creativity and "all the great events of time" starting "Within a moment: a pulsation of the artery." For Blake imagination is divine, inseparable from life itself. Kabbalah takes us to depths and heights beyond visual images, Ein Sof, no limit, infinity of infinity. For many, such words arouse a sensation that reverberates through one's being. A verbal sensation image that takes us beyond what can be imagined, opens us in ways we could not know.

For me, the term "sense" has special significance. It is one of those uniting words that spans psycho-spiritual dimensions. Sense as in vital sensing. Sense as in the various senses, hearing, seeing, touch, taste, smell, proprioception, interoception, kinaesthesia, all of which open worlds of experiencing, add colour to life, add life to life. One could add inner sensations associated with breathing, digestion, sexuality (Eigen, 1993, for depictions of experience and identity formations associated with breathing and appetite).

Sense associated with common sense. Sense associated with meaning. Sense associated with judgment and evaluation, good sense, bad sense. A sixth sense associated with intuition, inner guidance, and direction. Sense is a term that runs through capacities and modes of experiencing (Eigen, 2004b, 2007).

With a slight transposition, sense terms can be used for psychic taste and smell. We taste, smell and touch each other's personalities, character, tone, essence. Freud wrote of consciousness as a sense organ for the perception of psychical qualities. A sense organ that has depth as well as surface and can hardly be located simply as "consciousness". Other forms of consciousness, perhaps, with tendrils and roots growing from the Unknown. Bion writes of an unobserved, unknown galactic centre or origin of the universe. We can transpose this to an unknown centre or root of personality, deeper than strata and densities of our identities.

Alan: "I've long felt an inscrutable point beneath who I think I am. Below all my identities, habits, cultural biases, self-images. In the old days, people spoke not only of being "the child of parents" but also "a child of God". I wonder. The myth of being born of God, the son of God. Didn't "son of God" long ago mean simply a human being, a mensch? But there is also this special point, an invisible dot, miniscule and infinite. In the centre of my chest. A kind of centre of centres.

"It's taken all this time to say it's deeper than all the monsters, deeper than the deformities, the horrors. Deeper than so many self and God images I know. We strain to get through images to this miniscule, illimitable point. I can try to, dare to say it now because room has been made for it. It's been waiting. I sensed it when I was upside down distorted. I saw insides everywhere—or maybe I saw my insides everywhere. Worlds of distorted mirrors. And underneath, a pure, miraculous centre I could not make room for.

"A sense that released me. Not for keeps. I'm still me. Warped, ragged me. But it gave me another reference point, safe from everything I was, waiting for an opening. I'm afraid to say it and wouldn't wish it on anyone—but maybe what I went through made it possible to clear a space for something a little different, something better.

"All the images of myself were warped. Images of others not much better, some worse. Now and then, I'd see someone and feel—now there is someone who makes me feel good. A good feeling out of nowhere now and then. But, more than anything, it was the luck of coming upon the invisible point beyond images that gave me a sense that life was possible. A new feel of life."

There is a place that, for a moment, releases you from yourself, from the tyranny of identity. William Blake says that states are eternal. Mystical, poetic and love literature abounds with forever moments, good infinities and bad infinities. Here, for Alan, a good infinity or perhaps infinity beyond good and evil re-centres his sense of what life feels like. A different sense of life.

It took five years after his last hospitalisation for Alan to go through fuller realisations of a "rebirth" sequence. Usually it is aborted or semi-aborted, much as many dreams end before they can complete a sequence, unable to sustain the tension (Eigen, 1986, 1992). He had tastes of it along the way, moments of opening, times when distortions were less menacing. But a fuller going through took longer.

Keri Cohen in one of my Bion classes spoke of the therapy relation being a kind of incubator. Experience incubates. It takes time for new life to grow, test the waters, see if it can live, if nutriment can sustain it, if it won't be blown away for good. This going through I call a rhythm of faith, a rhythm at once sustained by faith that gives birth to faith. Always partial perhaps, but with a sense of a deeper whole even in fragments. It is an important turning point in one's sense of life, what life feels like. The great unknown that decimates you one moment, opens new dimensions of experiencing the next. Common language has many images for this, e.g., ups and downs, waves and roads, roller-coaster of emotions, darkness-light, obstruction-clearing, trapped-free, gestation-birth, negative-positive, struggle-grace. I tend to feel it as a basic structure of existence, an experiential rhythm.

Alan: "When I was taken to the hospital, there was only negative. No, that's not quite right. Things were mixed even then. I could not make use of the mix. There was life outside, a world outside the bad stuff coming at me, a world beyond the monstrous things. But I could not make use of it. I saw there was more but it was not real enough. What was really real was the bad thing, the awful thing. The ghastly faces around me. I did not associate them with my own soul. I always felt something rotting, sick in me. A feeling I didn't know what to do with. There didn't seem to be a place for it anywhere. But when I saw it coming at me from outside I didn't link up the two. Nothing held except the outside horror. That was real. There was nothing else real enough to compete with it.

"Slivers of soul images became real everywhere. But I lacked con-viction to oppose its momentum. I couldn't do anything to stop its momentum. I could not locate any part of it inside me. It's taken all this time for inside-outside channels to grow. Then it was all outside, only outside. And God knows there's enough outside bad and evil to reinforce that perception."

A fall into negative infinity evoked from the outside. An abyss of negative infinity within that could only be accessed by outside horrors. Perhaps part of the function of war is to bring home agony we lack equipment to access—as if outside horrors awaken us to the role our psychic makeup plays in creating them. Alan was magnetised by, glued to negative infinities. Over time, with therapy incubation, he began to feel more realities outside them, positive infinities and just plain ins and outs of ordinary existence.

What one moves towards is not elimination of the negative. That, perhaps, is only for saints, if at all possible or desirable. One moves towards a frame of reference capable of encompassing diverse tenden-cies in a more mutually nourishing way. As I wrote in *The Psychotic Core*, alternate infinities offset each other and, to a degree, modulate one another, add to the richness of living. It was not simply the magnified, gripping, overwhelming nature of negative perceptions (hallucinations) that almost did Alan in. That was bad enough. But also important was loss of modulating contact with offsetting tendencies that lost their sense of reality. Among other things, this brings home how important our frame of reference is for experience. If it is flexible and wide enough, many tendencies can be situated in relation to one another that otherwise could heighten self-injury.

This applies in more attenuated ways to less severe situations. A number of people have told me dreams about being trapped in a tower or irresistibly falling into freezing water through a hole in the ice. Tower, associated with head, top of the body. The body a freezing hole, the warmth frozen, chilled by life. For some, the balance of chilling life to warm life is skewed by chill. Not life-giving water, but water that menaces, threatens, kills.

What kind of body-mind, top-bottom connection is hinted at? On the one hand, trapped in schizoid isolation in a tower one can't get out of, sealed off from the frozen sea within. On the other, dreadful fear turned to ice. Alan had such dream images and, putting together remarks made on several occasions, said: "When I was a child I was afraid of everything. Once when playing outside—I must have been about four—the playground burst into flames. The whole world must have been on fire. I didn't scream. I didn't say a word. I sat and watched. And watched. And watched. My body paralysed. I could not, dare not move.

"I must have known I was seeing things that others weren't, although I wondered, did they see it too? Did everyone keep this a secret? Something we dare not mention. A silent agreement to pretend it wasn't there? Something too hot to go near that was consuming everything?

"The young woman who took care of me took my hand and we began walking home. I knew something happened to me but didn't know what. Something froze, sealed off and I became a watch-tower, a watcher. Not all sealed off but afraid. I knew something was wrong but didn't know what to do about it. Some people would think I'm crazy but the truth is I was lucky to break down and come here and begin to let the freeze thaw. The fire burst through the ice."

Therapy works with the fire a little at a time.

CHAPTER THREE

Fermenting devils in psychosis

L et me say right off that whatever I say is a tiny portion of what may be found, a selection from a pool without measure which can be jumped into or watched from an infinity of places. If I sound dogmatic or too sure at any point, know that anything I say is partial, qualified, subject to more swims and swimmers. What I will speak about is what I or others experienced and thought about. No claims other than aspects of psychic reality seemed one or another way for a shorter or longer time. Language and image play a role and so does a shifting sense of real-unreal.

Some of the people I write about have appeared before in my books and papers. More happens each time I dip into the feel of a person. Each time writing happens, more happens. Patients go on speaking in a therapist's soul after therapy ends.

There are many kinds and gradations of psychoses. Here I am most interested in certain happenings many share: the fact that it is not unusual for individuals who go mad—or hover on the verge of madness—to fear the devil. As I wrote in "On demonized aspects of the self" (Eigen, 1993), some say that God is dead, but for many the devil is very much alive.

29

To see devils and hear their commands is a dreadful thing. Good and evil become inextricably fused and one can't tell the difference between God and the devil. God may tell a person he will go to hell forever if he does not kill his brother or jump in front of a subway train. If one waits and does not act, in time one may find out Satan was disguised as God. Many people feel like cowards for not following such commands. It may take much therapy work to reach a point where one values one's wish to survive in face of such awful pressures. I almost wrote in face of such awful inner pressures. But the negative voice and vision have a cosmic aura that cannot simply be located as "mine".

It may be an unconscious sense of evil that manifests in evil visions-voices. For some, it is all too conscious and one is permeated by a felt conviction of being evil. One cannot always tell what part of the circle is the head or tail of the snake. Intense guilt can mushroom into hallucinatory hells and internal persecution can exacerbate guilt. A sense of evil has a long history in human culture, as does evil itself.

I have worked with many people who are not psychotic but who feel hugely guilty over small infractions, often sexual. One is not supposed to feel guilty about sex today, but guilt and anxiety play roles in many sexual conflicts. To be impaled on self-recrimination can be excruciating. Upbringing plays a role but so does unyielding unconscious structures. Life can be stained by a sense of being unforgivable.

One young woman spoke about "scruples", a code word for something in her that refused to have sex, condemned her for wanting to. Many psychoanalysts have written about an anti-libidinal force, the depths of which is immeasurable. Another berated herself for going to her friend's wedding in a setting her religion forbade. She was certain God was displeased and angels were crying. Pierre Janet wrote about a man's guilt over an extra-marital affair that led to a psychotic break needing hospitalisation (McCurdy, 1961). Janet struck up conversations with the voices that were attacking the man. Janet tried to open the possibility of learning more about them, who they were, what they wanted, in an attempt to ameliorate the patient's condition. Freud said that he took an individual's guilt over destructive wishes seriously, even if destructive acts were not discernible. The state of one's soul may be enough to make one feel horrible for who one is, especially in face of impotence to be otherwise.

In *The Psychotic Core* (1986; Elkin, 1972) I wrote of a division, even split, between an occultly transcendent mental self and fusional-explosive body self. A kind of hostile omniscience that thinks itself above and looks down and body feeling that mounts and explodes. Akin to a two- or three-year-old who wants to be good but periodically can't help a tantrum. Splits between watching-acting and being good-bad take dramatic turns in psychosis.

P-1 spoke of scoffing in his head, a mocking tone. He feared a devil had taken possession of his brain. I called this devil a "heh-heh" devil, which seemed to fit. His father died and his mother was permanently hospitalised in his teens. When he visited her she offered to "service" him. He was hospitalised with severe depression several times before we started to work.

In sessions he called himself evil, a devil, and a ghoul. He said, "Devils ferment in me. Inside there is a fermentation machine. Not a machine. Fermentation is alive. Devils and ghouls are super-alive. They attack my life, scare the living daylights out of me. Scare me to death. A farm inside that ferments devils. Devils ferment *me*. I look at them and see me. I am one of them but not only them. I am evil in my own right and my evil attracts."

He confessed over and over things he did that haunted him, a main one being putting his penis into the mouth of a baby decades ago. He could not get past that, did not want to. It was unforgivable. He spoke about it endlessly. Did something in him think the act would make him feel big, clean, pure? Did he know he would be haunted for life? It was something unspeakable, an urge that pushed him over the edge. He could not help himself. Maybe something to do with vulnerability of the baby, defenceless, like he once was, subject to ghastly pain inflicted by a mad mother's compromised boundaries. He cried and cried. Inside he was screaming. Body amorphous, head biting. But it was his body he could not stop. His head egged him on, a little like getting someone to do the dirty work for it. Evil thoughts, evil deeds. How can one live with this? Whatever thoughts he had to stop it—don't do it—were not strong enough. The urge to put his penis in the baby's mouth carried him over.

I think of the words, "Your sins will be white as snow." How? How does one start again, fresh, a new soul?

P-2: "I dig as deep as I can. Some kind of digging thing, not clear what, going deeper, deeper, through the earth's centre, its insides, my insides. There's a bad thing I'm trying to get to, trying to get out. I can't reach it.

"I've reached it thousands of times and rip at it and tear it out for a while but it comes back. Harsh, ugly, evil. It leaves no peace. It says: I'm the real you.

"I wonder, is this so? I used to feel everything was phony—like in the Bible, hypocrites. Only evil is real. I believe that but something in me won't let me believe it totally. I swing back and forth—evil, good, both. I don't know. There is no place to go with this. It doesn't stop. It's better not to try to solve it. Let it be."

Jewish mysticism speaks of good and evil inclinations. One side of the heart evil, one good. Like alchemy, there are visions of sublimation, transformation. William Blake tended to see Satan as energy and called energy "eternal delight". For him, Jesus was creative imagination. Put them together and you have creative imagination working with "satanic" energy, transformational existence. A sense of happy ending, a life of creative joy.

What are some traditional possibilities? One is evil is ignorance, transcended by knowledge. Another is evil as lack of good (*privatio boni*), a deficiency problem. Saint Paul felt his experience did not fit these models: I can't do what I want to do but do what I don't want to do. He is helpless to realise the good of his vision, falling prey to limitations and evil motives. His "solution" is an experience of grace in which such difficulties vanish, no longer relevant. In moments of grace he does not know what is body, spirit, mind—one simply lives in grace itself.

I find this a most profound happening, an important experiential core, an Archimedean reference point that once felt is as insistent and permeating as the evil core, even a potential framework for the latter. I called it Saint Paul's "solution" but it is a spontaneous happening, not willed. A "solution" from the depths perhaps, an alternative arising of an experiential dimension previously dormant. Akin to Buddha's sitting with suffering, samsara. At a certain point a surprising dimension opens, nirvana.

Melanie Klein (1946) seems to posit a double core or nucleus, good and bad experience, good and bad objects within, love and hate, creative and destructive tendencies. For Winnicott (1988; Eigen, 2009, 2014c), aggression is part of our tissue, part of our love, a necessary part of our verve for life. He feels its fate depends on how it is met, how it is related to. Part of feeling oneself bad hinges on quality of welcome, although there is no lack of ways that things can go wrong.

In one or another way, Freud posited an excitatory drive meeting inhibition, a model rooted not only in traditional culture and child rearing, but in the brain models he studied in the Gymnasium of his day. The old brain a basis for arousal, drive, sexual-aggressive push, the cortex selecting-inhibiting. Tensions of systems intrinsic to the way we work.

The idea of excitations striving for satisfaction, pushing the personality to seek relief or heightened pleasure is ancient, hierarchies of lower-higher capacities part of spiritual and philosophical discourse. There are many variations on the work of capacities, existence levels and transformational aspirations. One of the streams (with many substreams) involves spontaneous arising of demon images. A favourite of mine is a sculpture in a Kyoto temple that I call a Buddha or Kwan Yin sandwich. Many Buddha demons are piled on top of one another, each on the head or shoulders of the one below it. At the very top is Kwan Yin (Kannon), bodhisattva of compassion, kindness. She is the foil or counterpart of Bion's force that can do nothing but destroy (Bion, 1965; Eigen, 1998). Kwan Yin can do nothing but be compassionate. Below her are all the demons, suggesting a primacy of compassion in the use of demonic energy, loosely akin to Blake's Jesus as creative imagination channelling satanic energy.

The nineteenth century saw an explosion of literary-philosophical images and ideas clustering around an excitatory power. A restless will to live (Schopenhauer) that cannot be satisfied and often results in evil acts to further its aims, the will to power (Nietzsche), and for some a creative power (Emerson, Wordsworth, Coleridge) that shapes existence. A sense of upsurge that can work for good or ill, partly depending on how they are met and shaped. Surges that, too often, we are helpless in face of as they toss us like rag dolls (a Taoist phrase) in the wind. The idea of control becomes something of a fetish when we cannot even name what drives us. Or, as Schopenhauer remarked, we may be able to exercise some control over our actions but cannot will what we want.

There was already a good deal of fascination with madness and evil in the cultural world that nourished Freud. Themes involving doppelgangers (an evil double), gothic literature with harvests of mad transformations—one could go on listing a growing fascination with unconscious forces that link madness and evil. Was Satan mad or sane? Two centuries earlier John Milton had Satan say, "Evil be thou my good." Was Satan merely a human mirror with exaggerated envy and pride and murderous will? Was Milton's drama a magnification of tendencies in everyday life, everyday madness and evil and good? Still earlier, Shakespeare's portrayals in which evil and madness slide into each other. Lady Macbeth's invocation of the spirits to cure her of compassion so that she can be more purely evil. Macbeth vainly hoping to help her, asking the physician, "Canst thou not minister to a mind diseased?" With hindsight, it appears no accident that Shakespeare's popularity mushroomed in the nineteenth century, the milieu that gave birth to Freud.

Freud lowered the number of drives to two, although their names changed somewhat in different writings. Sex and aggression, hunger and reproduction (self-preservation, race-presentation), life drive-death drive. I'm not sure any term of Freud's has become more popular than libido, which commonly is used to mean sex drive. For Freud, at times, linked with the god Eros, it seemed almost a cosmic force as well. I've felt, at times, it was partly a cocaine vision which got somewhat whittled down to fit semi-scientific, literary and common discourse. At one time or another, it seems that any of the main psychic divisions can be driven and function as a driving force, pushing and pulling personality in complex ways. Tension within and between systems seemed almost a rule for Freud, a model characteristic of ancient philosophy and modern neurology.

While Freud stated that psychoanalysis arose as a treatment for neurosis, not psychosis, it does not take much to see the influence of psychotic phenomenology in the structure of his work. Freud was no stranger to hospitals and asylums and made good use of his exposure to Charcot and Bernheim in France, which formed a background for his own speculations about hysteria. He later developed a structural theory in which aspects of psychosis play a major, implicit role (Eigen, 1986, 2010, 2012, 2014c). For example, he describes the id as a seething cauldron of excitations where the law of contradiction does not hold, the early ego a hallucinatory organ developing anti-hallucinatory aspects over time, the superego prone to overdoing it, persecuting personality. Over the span of his work, Freud wrote of mad aspects of love, identification with parents and leaders, idealisation and transference phenomena, and what seemed like inescapable war.

Inherent in the theory are conflicts between yes and no. Tendencies that refuse to take no for an answer but must, or go haywire because no no is effective, or no is too cruel or strangulating. How various personality tendencies work together or fail to becomes raw material for creative portrayals of who and what we are and how we develop. Even the ego, attached to perceptual and social reality, is conceived as a hallucinatory organ as well, a double agent, pressed by a need for truth and delusion. We feel our struggle for sanity in Freud's work but if we look just a little closer, we feel how mad we are too.

I mention in *The Psychotic Core* (1986) that Freud, in part, rewrote the notion of sin as madness and neurosis. To be sure, that was not entirely novel. Biblical writers and early church fathers referred to God as the great Physician. Evil, sin and madness were intertwined elements of human disease needing help. God was looked on as cure but it did not escape notice that God created an external-internal world in which torments breed. Soul-sickness was a term already in use, semi-popularised by William James, a phrase also used for will and spirit.

It was not entirely novel that dialogue became an avenue of "cure", or at least ameliorative interaction. There are medieval accounts of madness helped through contact with good words or face and, I suspect, biblical healings, while exaggerated into fables, had enough kernels of truth to alert us to the power of human interaction for good and ill (Eigen, 1986).

It did not take long before psychoanalysts became engaged with psychosis, starting to see neurosis and perversion as defences against psychotic anxieties. I once heard Henry Elkin say at a talk at the New School in the 1960s, "Behind every neurosis is a hidden psychosis." Melanie Klein, Winnicott, R. D. Laing, Marion Miler, Bion, Harry Stack Sullivan, Harold Searles—psychoanalytic concern with madness came out of the closet. Book titles like *The Suppressed Madness of Sane Men* (Milner, 1987), *On Private Madness* (Green, 1996)—more than hints of something opening up. Madness was not just an aberration of the few but part of the human condition, often playing a semi-invisible role in destructive scenarios, but sometimes helpful as well.

It was often said that psychoanalysis made us less responsible for our actions, since evil was now seen as disease, psychological ill health requiring treatment. This seems to me a popular misunderstanding, often fuelled by analysts themselves. First of all, psychoanalysis is an odd kind of treatment, since we never know how well it will do in any particular case. I am told by physicians who treat serious illness that such is a fact in their work as well. Secondly, psychoanalysis is an instrument that is largely unknown to itself, engaged in exploration of what it is and can do. Bion likens it to a baby or embryo in process of development, capacities as yet to grow. Already we can help people once called mad, at least some of the time, to some extent. Not as much or as reliably as we would like. But inroads have been made.

Thirdly, psychoanalysis itself is a "symptom" of humanity, an emergent phenomenon that signals aspects of psychosocial life that are swimming into view. What does its very existence say about who we are, how we feel and taste to ourselves? Psychoanalysis as a new form of self-interest, awareness of the importance of emotional realities largely unknown. Emotional realities we live and that live us. An evolving way of sensing our existence.

To see it as closing responsibility is to misrecognise where it might take us, since dimensions of human responsiveness are part of its field of exploration. This includes attending to how we experience ourselves, how we *can* experience ourselves. And the paradox that as we pay attention, the field of experience we attend to grows in complexity. The capacity of attention itself undergoes development. To realise that whatever we notice occurs in a larger field that may remain unknown is not only chastening but thrilling, opening possibility of compassionate humility in face of the vast depths of life.

Years ago I was told about a catatonic patient in a hospital sitting in one place for fifteen years. Sitting perfectly still for fifteen years is impossible. I don't know how eating took place—spoon fed by others, a tube, intravenously or sometimes he ate himself?

My picture: he was eating himself alive inside until nothing or less than nothing was left. The more he ate, the more appeared, until he was eating on dimensions of invisible nothings. Eating one's psychical insides has no end.

He may not have been totally still in one place the whole time. But from what I was told, his body was stiff and still for long periods. Then after fifteen years he came to, started out of it, and began to move. He was rusty and had to dip into body movements a little at a time. Moving naturally took practice and he never fully lost his stiffness. When questioned, he reported a dramatic shift in an inner crisis. For years he was paralysed by perception and thought oscillating around a central dilemma: was the universe basically good or evil. One moment good, one moment evil. He could not decide or, better, a decision could not be reached. It was a dilemma that extended to all humanity, all life—were human beings basically evil or good? Was life basically evil or good? He was petrified in dread that everything was basically evil, in which case he and all life would and should perish. Just as he was almost absolutely sure it was evil, a hint of good saved the day. Now this way, now that. Each moment's position final, yet each containing the other, turning into the other.

He does not know how it happened but he became aware of an inner change, a shift of internal atmosphere. A decision was made. Had it been building? Was it sudden? It was decided that life was basically good. Evil was real but so was goodness and, ultimately, evil could not destroy all goodness. Goodness in some form, in some way, would survive evil. A profound internal happening that made life feel different. Goodness might vanish but something began to trust in its return, that it would subsist.

Jewish mysticism echoes this situation, saying if, for a moment, all goodness should vanish, the universe instantaneously would be destroyed. Or, again, if not for several good men in any era, the universe would end in a moment. No goodness, no universe, no life, no humanity. I suspect this saying reflects something going on within us, an inner crises of essential importance. Something in us must feel that life is basically good or suffer catastrophic destruction. Perhaps only our illusion of good is destroyed? Or something more, catastrophic breakdown of personality.

As Pontius Pilate asked, "What is truth?" We could ask, "What is goodness?" We could focus on goodness and bring out many meanings in many contexts, including evil use of good. Plato resorted to an ineffable Idea of the Good, the Form of the Good that informs all particular manifestations of goodness. Perhaps it was his way of preserving a good nucleus in face of massive inner and outer attacks on the idea or reality of goodness. Perhaps it was his way of trying to stay sane. Yet isn't the ability to see through goodness to the evil it masks part of sanity, down to earth cynical perception of reality? I once remarked that one must include pessimism but opt for optimism. One must see the hypocrisy of goodness and through it realities of evil, but that is not the end of it, that does not foreclose the goodness of goodness. It might be good to make useful definitions here, but that is beyond me. We are left with intuitive sensing with all its dangers. We are left with whatever made the catatonic man come down on the side of yes, without precluding no.

P-2: "Back and forth, good and evil, yes and no. I *was* stuck in devil land, no way out. Except life did not confine itself to being stuck. *I* was stuck but not only stuck. I did not spend all my waking hours in the hospital being terrified. I did not see devils all the time. I hung out with other people, some really interesting. I met a woman. I made a friend. One of the doctors touched my life feeling. I felt better being with him, nothing in particular we said. You never knew when a devil would appear. You could see devils in some people more of the time. Sometimes I thought someone was a devil. You can't imagine the fright unless you've felt it. Something in me was stuck there, but something wasn't. I never stopped being enthralled by great blue skies."

When he said he was digging to get the bad thing out of him, I thought of the holes drilled into skulls of pre-historic man. Was that a procedure to let the bad thing out? What does one do with the bad thing, the worm in the rose, the rotten thing in the state?

P-3: "What I do is live with it. A big difference from the time I started here. The devil faded. Flare ups come but now I know good feelings come again. I can wait it out."

This man and I went through a lot. We spoke with the voices and, when it was possible, I encouraged him to focus on the devil image and see what happens to it. With repeated attempts he began to see changes, see other people in the devil's face, see his own face in the devil mirror. Images transform with repeated attention, but getting to that place isn't easy. With some people in this predicament, I sometimes can lead them to feel the devil energy all through their body, or a bit at a time, let the excitation spread, let the body come alive in new ways. Instead of the excitation turning immediately into a terrifying devil, it turned into moments of fuller aliveness.

P-2: "But there are moments when it feels worse than ever. I'm convinced I've been fooling myself. The bottom line is the fact of evil. No exceptions. I'm evil and that is everlasting, the final word. Total fear, horror.

"When I was a kid I saw witches in my bedroom window in the middle of the night and turned the lights on. My parents got annoyed but in time let me be. If I needed a light on, they no longer shut it off. I'm kidding myself thinking there is anything but eternal hell. But at least I *can* kid myself and go on with the day most of the time. I can act as if goodness was real. I can make believe. I read somewhere that if you can act as if a good feeling is real, then it must be real somewhere in you or you would not even be able to fake it."

P-2, to my knowledge, never needed hospitalisation again and eight months after leaving the hospitalisation preceding seeing me, took himself off medication. Some people may need medication for longer periods, some all their lives. But some are unable to live with it and would rather suffer the beings they are without it. In his case, P-2 came through his suffering and made a go of it, enduring difficult states when they pressed.

Somewhere Paul Tillich wrote: a man is only as big as the diabolic in himself he can assimilate. Sometimes engaging and making use of psychic attack is growth producing. Sometimes it is enough just to get through it. I remember a man telling me about a bad LSD experience, so bad he could only get under his covers in bed and wait for it to pass. Other times, an image or feeling might blow him apart, or lift him to another level. One special time he went outside at night high on acid and to his amazement the ordinary people he saw on the street had beautiful souls. He could see the basic goodness in each person, no matter what distortions their personalities underwent in order to survive. This moment became part of a new psychic underpinning, a frame of reference large enough to situate many blows.

Fairbairn (1954) talked about therapy as a kind of exorcism of structures in which excitement and rejection fuse. With luck, good experiences can partly assimilate and ameliorate the excitement-rejection cycle, a fusion that can have demonic force, mixtures of excitement devils and rejection devils, caught in wounds and self-wounding.

P-1: "Is this fermentation or the opposite of fermentation? Did I dream this? See it? A devil inside hard ice. I say ice because I feel the chill. As I say this, I want to talk of the oneness of ice and fire, but that's not what I mean. I think of the plague of hail in the Passover Seder and inside the centre of the hail is hardened fire, fire and brimstone. No— my devil is in ice.

"I get the urge to crack it. I am trying to crack it. I bang it on something, a table. It's not hard enough. I need a steel floor or table or wall. I bang it against the steel, harder, harder. It does not crack. It is harder than steel and colder.

"It is inside me. It lives inside the ice in my heart. It controls me, taunts me from the ice inside my heart. Remote control deep in my insides. I think of the prophet: turn hearts of stone to flesh. I think of the saying, the reality: God is closer to you than you are. But with me, the devil is closer. The devil in his house of ice. Why do they always picture the devil as fire? Because ice burns?

"Ice burns inside my heart. Is this another kind of fermentation, fermenting a heart of ice?"

Freud has written that perhaps even earlier than repression is reversal (Freud, 1911c; Green, 1996; Eigen, 1986). Reversal can work many ways, e.g., reversals of affect, pronoun (subject-subject, subject-object), and direction. Love can turn into hate and hate into love. Love can defend against or mask hate and hate can defend against and mask love. I can be you, you can be me. I may attribute emotional states to you that belong to me and claim emotions as mine that belong to you. Love or hate can turn outward or inward, e.g., turning against the self.

This operation or dynamism can work in many domains. Gestalt psychology charts reversals of figure-ground, or figure-figure. For example, staring at a figure in a picture that one moment looks like a girl, the next a witch or death head. It is, I feel, a phenomenon with wide application. God—no God, self—no self, sensitive—insensitive, yes—no, hot-cold emotions, near-far, towards-away. The list can be multiplied (Eigen, 2011b).

In the cases above, devil—no devil, evil-goodness. It may even be that the fact of reversibility gives cause for realistic hope in some therapies. Freud noted that we pass through something like psychotic states at night in dreams, but recover in the morning. He wondered if the amazing reversibility of states of sleeping and waking mind might not hold out hope for working with psychosis.

Freud packed double, multiple states and functions in his concept of libido, which could be stuck in some ways, flowing in others. Attaching, "cathecting" diverse objects and subjects, capable of condensation-displacement. He likened it to electrical, liquid flow, which implies it can short-circuit, start a fire, freeze, flood—states that patients in this paper experienced. One sees, too, affinities between libido and serpents and dragons in Asian spirituality, the antics of Greek gods, and the all too predictable mishaps in the Bible (which when they happen are experienced as shocks). Libido as electrocuting-electrifying or simply pleasurable-painful.

In later phases, Freud (1937c) paid increasing attention to stuck libido, blockages, even "lazy", inert or stagnant libido. From early on, he used the term "fixation" to note stuck points. Later, the notion of being stuck, blocked, stagnant grew to virtually encompass much of one's living being (a notion already inherent in early formulations of "psychasthenia", weakened libido, but which deepened and extended in later preoccupation with death-work; Eigen, 1996).

The coupling, plasticity-rigidity, was a significant concern of Freud's and also my patients. On the one hand they were mired in a position they could not get out of. A position they likely were in a long time and did not know it. As psychosis begins to break out in more florid form, individuals often feel they can control it, make it stop. They also are terrified that something terrible is happening to them. There usually comes a time, often in hospital, when it dawns on them that they cannot make it stop, they do not control it. Help then becomes more of a possibility.

The people I write of here eventually reached that point and more, not only realising they could not help themselves get out of it, but they were profoundly stuck in something rigid and unyielding. It was as if the excitatory and inhibitory drives or functions Freud described (id, ego, superego) were maximally, relentlessly fused, a kind of hyperexcitation and rigor-mortis of personality, braking and accelerating at the same time. The result: paralysis. Blood-curdling, chilling paralysis made of merciless persecution in the form of devils. At once boiling and freezing, afire and frozen in hell. As one person put it, icy heart and fevered soul. It is not possible to describe the chilling terror these people lived before ice began to break up and pieces thaw, before fire became less of an incinerator (imagine: incessant electrocution, drowning, freezing, cremation while alive). I must say, I truly feel these states go on within us now, to variable degree, and we are challenged to know what to do with them.

As mentioned earlier, I often try, slowly by degrees, to help a person look at the devils, feel them, taste them, speak with them. This is not always possible. A lot depends on long-term being together, not simply what is said, but the feel of being in the same room together that grows over time. A bond perhaps or just the feel of the other person growing familiar. Moments of wellbeing unpredictably happen between the cracks and gradually a person begins to look forward to them and they grow. It's still scary but over time a taste for therapy develops. To adapt an image Freud took from Weber describing dreams: therapy as another scene where madness finds a place. Where reversibility has more room: I am evil—I am not evil, I am and am not evil. Little by little, new relationships with the feeling of being evil forms. More, a growing relationship with more possibilities of movement begins with what might be the real evil within.

We are speaking of gruelling work in the trenches but there are moments where one can jump levels and, for a time, be in the clear. Here is an example from work with a dying woman, who one moment felt herself evil, another felt attacked by evil presences.

At the same time, she realised her own emotional states were tormenting her. She had periods of hospitalisation in her life, but that was over twenty years earlier. As part of her attempt to heal, she became a kabbalah student and teacher. She had long been involved in spirituality but only later in life felt strongly attracted to kabbalah studies. There was room in kabbalah for the extreme and varied states she experienced, hells and heavens that were excruciating and ecstatic homes.

She was a gifted teacher, profoundly intuitive. At the same time, she could fall victim to mind spins, a spinning mind she sometimes likened to a washing machine, except instead of cleaning her inner clothes it ripped them and made them filthier. Bad thoughts without end, infinities of bad thoughts she feared would trap her forever, trapped by the evil within, personal and cosmic. No matter how hard she tried, she could not get out of these states when they assailed her and gathered momentum. Meditation at such moments was too terrifying. She was gripped beyond endurance.

She complained from time to time that her mind was also an eraser. One moment it was screeching chalk on a blackboard, next it erased all the lines and she was blank. Now she prayed, if only it would blank out the horrible accusations, the devil accuser, and sense of damnation. She was petrified her last state would be hellish and she would be condemned to remain in her last state forever.

It brought some relief to speak of all the evil things she did, all the evil she thinks she caused, things for which she can never be forgiven, for which she could not forgive herself. Another hell: the impossibility of forgiveness.

She had a threatening illness for much of her adult life, with many years of relative remission, but now in her seventies, it grew worse, and toxic side effects of treatment were mounting. She was in hospice for several months. As death neared, she voiced over and over her dread of dying in an unbearable state that would last forever.

The last times we spoke it came to me to speak about yechida, a soul dimension that is at all times in contact with God, essence to essence, a soul point of which the psalms say, "The soul I have given you is pure." There are five souls in Chassidus-Kabbalah (Eigen, 2012, 2014a, 2014b), each with their qualities and states, torment being part of lower soul regions, but also distributed through other systems. The yechida soul—oneness—is, I feel, generally above the fray, beyond the torment, a pure soul essence linked with God's essence, heart to heart, being to being. Instead of my usual advice to go into what you feel, the state of the moment, I told her, "Go higher, higher, above. Beyond the torment, into yechida."

She was a kabbalah mystic and knew exactly what I meant, instantaneously and fully. In seconds I heard her breathing grow slower, even, and quiet. I spoke with her on Tuesday and said we would speak again Thursday morning. When I called, I learned that she passed away in peace.

I was very grateful and felt peace spread through me as well. We are not always so lucky. I think of P-2 saying after experiencing a relatively devil free time: "Waxing and waning like the moon. He (the devil) has faded and for the moment I do not feel evil. It is a bliss to feel what God said when he created the universe—it is good. For the moment. If I've learned anything, it swings back and forth. Now here, now not. What is real? The goodness, the evil? Both, neither? I don't know. But I'm grateful for this moment."

CHAPTER FOUR

Where is body?

W hat is body? For Saint Paul, in moments of grace, categories dissolve. Words like body and mind do not hold. The "where" of where one is, is ineffable.

In *Lust* (2006a), I write of moments when sensation is ineffable. In such moments, sensation is not simply a Platonic step up the ladder to higher spirit, it is itself ineffable reality opening realities.

My little contribution to this discussion is meant to be suggestive, without definitions. I've never been able to define anything. But, if lucky, we can touch or tease some echoes of experience. I think of God asking great biblical figures, "Where are you?" To which they reply, "I am here." Where is this here? Do they speak from the fear or love of their hearts? Do they mean the here of existence? Surely they are not speaking of a Google map.

As soon as we begin to "name" body organs we are involved with spiritual reality. Heart is perhaps foremost, good heart, bad heart. Spiritual "systems" even locate good and evil in heart chambers. Chassidic literature speaks of the good inclination on the right side of the heart, the evil on the left. Hindu writings speak of a special heart on the right side of the chest that is a place of spirit.

We could name many organs low-high, front-back, right-left, and their psycho-spiritual correlates in one or another system, e.g., chakras, sephirot (Eigen, 2012, 2014a, 2014b). Terms like body ego, body subject, body spirit, body soul, astral body, reverberate with multiple realities that colour life. The Bible says the soul is in the blood, which D. H. Lawrence echoes.

The more we feel our bodies, the more there is to feel. As a young man in a bio-energetic class, the leader tried an intervention in which I lay over his back, back on back, and he pulled me up, off the ground, and bent slightly forward, so that my back stretched and arched, a bow. I did not expect what happened. When he asked what I felt, I said, "Like a vagina." My whole body became a vagina. You might say, an imaginary vagina. But at that moment I was filled with ineffable sensation that brought me to another reality. I am tempted to use a Bion notation and say, I got a taste of O-itself, all through my body, which opened dimensions of experience I did not know before (Bion uses O as a notation for unknown ultimate reality, here emotional-sensory).

In roughly the same time period, in my mid-twenties, I was doubled over in pain on a bus. Where was the pain? Stomach? Heart? Gut? Not in any tangible location? It was the pain of my life. I went into it, felt it and felt it, doubled over, gripping myself. At some point, I blanked out, and in the darkness a field of light opened, wondrous light, lifting existence, opening being.

Momentous moments, becoming a vaginal being, seeing the light. Reference points that transform the feel of life.

When I was young, there was little difference between Eros and spirit, except when acute guilt provoked tormenting difference. Now as an old man, there are moments when body turns into veils fluttering gently, tissues in velvet darkness through which ineffable dimensions with no names open, wave after wave.

It is not that body vanishes, more that it fades, softens, and more happens. Whatever the discontinuities, there is also fluidity between dimensions.

Here is one moment, in which a certain "flow" occurred between dimensions of experience. Kirk rubbed his shoulder and spoke of a pain he felt just under the joint ball, where it meets torso. After a time the pain spreads into chest and he speaks of heart pain, now rubbing his chest. I am aware he is under treatment for elusive physical difficulties and wait it out. He said something hard to hear about "ghosts", pains as ghosts, as they slid from shoulder through chest.

I had a series of nearly simultaneous thoughts, sensings, visions. Pains as ghosts of emotional trauma, mute impacts seeking-resisting acknowledgement. Ways the stress of feeling from infancy on pinch nerves, bones, muscles, organs. Bion (1994) says the core of a dream is an emotional experience. Our body is an emotional body and language is an emotional language. We lack capacity to work with feeling well and tend to suffer from partial emotional indigestion. We do not know what kind of pain is being dealt with how. I feel my breath has gotten somewhat shorter and faster as if feeling Kirk's pain a little.

When I came back into focus (the above thoughts a kind of day-dream) I hear Kirk speaking of the pain of life. Agony felt all lifelong as part of existence. The shoulder pain he came in with dissolved into pain hard to localise and what he called his heart liquefied. He spoke of pain as a kind of pool in the centre of his chest that radiated out-ward through a psychic body. At this point, what some call physical, emotional, psycho-spiritual meld. Kirk broke into tears and in moments was sobbing from his heart. But what heart? The physical organ? Emo-tional organ? Spiritual pain?

Here is another example of fluid transformational processes working across dimensions with a man, Harry, who sought help after several hospitalisations. He eventually became hospital and medication free (Eigen, 2007, Chapter Three). The momentary level and tone was dif-ferent from Kirk's, but one feels interplays between inner-outer realities that touch feeling and bring spirit to another place.

Harry felt his words killed people but he was stymied because he did not see anyone die when he spoke. He felt he had no impact. He would begin to die out and watch his emotional self go under.

At the time I wish to share, we were sitting quietly, listening to our breathing. There is noise outside. My office is on the ground floor fac-ing the street. A child cries and a mother chastens it, a delivery man chains his bicycle to the bars of my window. Harry breaks into tears, weeps and weeps, sobbing thoroughly for the first time and says, "The mother yelling at the child was too much. When I heard the bike chains I thought, she is chaining the child. I have an urge to step outside and breathe, to unchain the child. I want to give that mother a softer voice. When I hear her voice I stop breathing. My soul stops breathing. My breath contracts around the pain. I'm breathing cautiously, breathing around the pain. My breath cushions the pain … now my chest is starting to relax. Soul is in my chest, returning through my chest."

I too cringed at the mother's metallic, scraping tone, my insides tightening, soul tightening, all through my body. A tongue lashing is a kind of beating. The emotional and physical meld. When Harry and I thawed out some, my hand involuntarily went to my heart. In one moment, spirit leaves, in another begins to return.

A few moments later, Harry fears that the child outside has stopped breathing. Does he mean a child within has lost spirit? We breathe around the pain, contract, find ways of surviving. For the moment, everything is in a breath. I think of the breath of life in the Bible, *ruach elohim*, God's breath-spirit enlivening life, enabling us to be.

There might be ways we stop breathing, never breathe again. Feeling has breath as well as taste buds. Our literal body might go on breathing in restricted ways, enough to get by, but emotional breath and taste may be damaged. Can you imagine a person who has stopped breathing emotionally? I have worked with people where this is so, and know places in myself where this is so. In Kabbalah, emotional life is associated with *ruach*, breath, emotional level of spirit (Eigen, 2012).

What is happening with Harry in the incident above? It is one moment in which he is coming alive in a new way, a moment in the birth of experience that spans dimensions, emotional soul awakening, heightening spirit. We are together resonating to sound, shrill yelling, metal chains. One moment binding, loss, another recovery. Sound runs through our bodies, giving birth to image, psychic sensing. Something is happening. The Bible links new birth with a child within. With Harry the child begins to thaw out and breathe with the going and coming of spirit, little bursts of time. We sit together, permeable, ready for more.

I'd like to add a word about images of up and down, e.g., dreams of being in the subway or flying in the air. One person felt his body a drill going into the ground, where he discovered a hidden subway system that no one knew but him. A magical world under the ground in which he could come and go as if invisibly. The same person also dreamt he could fly, so that his body was amphibian, now below the earth, now above it.

Flying and living underground express a need to escape the pain of living on earth. But they are more, suggesting also the life of spirit, including our double sense of being both above and below. Eyes as a centre of consciousness above, mouth and body with centres below (e.g., heart, gut, genital mind-spirit). We are made of multiple centres of experience. Ascent-descent is one of a number of organisers. We both subtend and transcend ourselves. Individuals report out of body experiences, on the one hand. While, on the other hand, attention can be placed on body surfaces and insides in ways that open infinities of feeling. The more one focuses on body areas, inside or out, the more nuances of being one discovers. Varying qualities of attention add to the taste and tone of experience.

Sensing has tended to be a second-class citizen in Western epistemology, low on the intellectual-spiritual scale. It is often taken for granted, that one transcends the senses to reach deeper dimensions of intuition and spiritual development. At the same time, sensation is a field of revelation, opening worlds that enrich one's sense of living. The term "sense" is one of those uniting words that run through multiple dimensions of experiencing: the five senses, a sixth sense, common sense, sense as meaning, and as Freud notes, consciousness as a sense organ for the perception of psychical qualities. Worlds that keep opening the more we open to them. One even may have a sense of God, a God sense with no end. We are all explorers of where head-heart-guts bring us, and much more (Eigen, 2014a, 2014b).

The body visible is mostly invisible. Feeling touches us from unknown places or no place at all. It is not easy to pin ourselves down and undulating waves of body feeling are part of life's elusiveness, a sense including the rise and fall of spirit that is part of a rhythm of faith.

CHAPTER FIVE

There is no no

"There is no no in the unconscious, says Freud," Bruce avows. "So it doesn't matter how much I say no in real life. I am still not saying no deep inside."

"I'm not sure what you mean by that, Bruce. Are you saying it doesn't matter what you do, you cannot get better?" I replied.

We give a big round look at each other, grazing in each other's gaze. Being with each other was fun at that moment. I thought of moments when mother-baby or lovers gaze at each other. Gaze and gaze.

It doesn't matter what you do, you can't get better. Two no's in our faces. It was like a card game. He played his no's, I mine.

What makes the baby-mother's gaze so beautifully infinite? A whole moment without end. A moment of beauty in its own right.

In the English language there is a funny accident: hole in whole. Part of the infinity of the gaze is the possibility that a hole will open and swallow it at any moment. It is perhaps all the more beautiful because in a blink it could be gone.

No matter what we say, no keeps appearing. It is part of the background of speech and like a jack in the box can pop out anytime.

52   IMAGE, SENSE, INFINITIES, AND EVERYDAY LIFE

BRUCE:	In real life, when people speak, no can mean yes and yes mean no. The line between them is not hard and fast.
M.E.:	"So there may be no yes in the unconscious either?"
BRUCE:	"I picture yes and no as sleds we slide on."
M.E.:	"We slide on each other?"
BRUCE:	"Into each other is more like it. I feel your no in me, your yes in me and I fear you will not be able to take my yes and no."
M.E.:	"Your indecision, make believe? Confusion?"
BRUCE:	"No, the hard thrust of yes or no, slippery or not. Like rocks thrown through a window."
M.E.:	"I'll crack? I'll break under the pressure of our being together?"
BRUCE:	"Yes, that comes closer. If we are too real, we will break."
M.E.:	"No and yes keep us unreal? Protects us?"
BRUCE:	"Isn't so much of life taking sides, making believe it really is this or that, believing it's yes or no?"

* * *

Digression 1: Moses and Korach

Korach challenged Moses's authority, said no to Moses. "Who are you to put yourself above us? Aren't we all holy?" (Numbers 16).

All Israel is holy. Was Moses baffled for a moment or did he see it coming? We know Moses had an anger "problem"—was he furious, this most humble of all men in God's service?

Buber (1958) sees Moses as a figure of struggle. One struggles to modulate the negative in oneself, destructive urges, psychopathic dominance, cruelty. One struggles to be a better person—the prophets' circumcision of the heart. *Korach* represents that aspect of personality that feels one should be and have everything without struggle, just as one is, no limitations (no no or, as mother used to say in a singsong way, no-no). Everything is perfect, just so, now.

Korach represented 250 men of the Hebrew elite, already above most others as priests. Rabbis sagely speculated that he wanted not simply equality but to be above Moses and Aaron, the top of the hierarchy, *numero uno*. Yet what he asserted and stood on was the truth that we are all equal before God and as God's children, God's bride, equal in holiness in essence, in truth, in reality. One might say that Moses represented doing, *Korach* being, intrinsic being.

There is a story that God offered the Torah to all the people of the
earth but when they heard what would be required, rejected it. Finally,
God offered it to the Hebrew people who said, "First we will do, then
ask." And so the *Ivri* became God's special people.

In another story (Leviticus 10:1), two of Aaron's sons sought to do
away with limitations and seek full contact with divinity, no barriers.
The story speaks of "strange" fire that does not follow rules and goes
straight to the goal region. They were burnt to a crisp by their own fire,
perhaps from closeness to the source (God's fire) they could not tolerate. In such a case, rules—yes and no regulations—act as filter systems
for divine energy and our own drives. Rules mediate meeting. Rules are
places of meeting. Rules attempt to regulate closeness-distance. How
close without getting burnt? Some might say this burning is glorious
and the story conveys the vanishing of the soul in heavenly union.

Moses fell to the ground and God provided the answer. The earth
opened under *Korach's* feet and he and his followers vanished on the
spot. Falling through the hole that was beneath them the whole time.
And yet we are given psalms by *Korach's* sons who not only survived
but grew in Holy Spirit.

Through rules we enter a place of nullity. What if I find myself in a
situation for which there are no rules or, at least, I don't know of any
(homonym: know-no)? When Bion finds himself in such a situation he
(1) makes his own rules (1994, p. 237) and/or (2) waits in unknowing, in
the middle of the fire and mindful witness-observer (1994, pp. 234–235).

There is a voice saying, "I have been burnt to a crisp many times,
over and over." And I have not—for in each case, the burning has been
aborted, partial.

The hole opening beneath us, within us, opens the problem (probe)
of nullification. Mystical nullification invites us to null ourselves in
God's service. Give ourselves to the Torah—don't kill, covet, steal, com-
mit adultery. One could add three more to reach the Noachide laws, six
more for the Ten Commandments, and hundreds towards the 613, and
then many rabbinic additions.

The laws of your own heart? We are told beware of your eyes and
heart lest they lead you astray. The eyes and heart of the evil inclination,
self-centred imagining. We are told half our heart is evil, half good and
in Hindu psychology we hear that the heart on the left is a lower nature,
the heart on our right higher. Not so easy to follow your heart, your
bliss—trouble is just around the corner or under you, waiting to open.

As Jesus hinted and Saint Paul amplified: have any of us been able to follow good commandments without blemish? Let he or she without sin, cast the stone. Yes, there is struggle. There had better be or we'd be even worse off than we are. But there is also grace, beyond or to the side, beneath or in the struggle: bliss, intimacy, love, relief beyond words.

Sometimes I divide the pool into three dimensions (Eigen, 2014b). (1) Just plain me—ordinary me living daily life. (2) Constant struggle— trying to make oneself a better being, appalled at the way one wounds those one loves, one's children, one's partner, one's self. Is there anything I can do to lessen inevitable destructiveness, daily injuries and murders? How offer effective opposition to myself, put into effect a helpful critique of being? (3) Grace—beyond the torment of binaries, beyond the struggle of right and wrong, a field of Grace. The three moments or tendencies inform and add to each other.

It may be that *Korach* wants #3 without #2. Or with a turn of mind, we might see in him a moment of mystical nullification that transcends law and struggle. Just for a moment, an everlasting moment that rings like a quiet bell through our beings. There is self-nullification in deference to the Law, and self-nullification beyond it. Both have dangers and potential benefits. A doubleness which in the life-space of planet Earth we may never get rid of.

Digression 2: You are my woman

In a discussion of full and empty speech, Lacan gives "You are my woman" (Lacan, 1993, pp. 36–37), as an example of full speech. He uses the word *fides*, faith, as in good faith, a term of self-commitment that commits the other as well—*you*—you are mine, my woman. As another example, "You are my master", and perhaps we can add, "You are my analyst". "Speech that gives itself", he calls it. To paraphrase loosely, "You are in my speech. I am speaking in your place, committing you, pledging both of us in certainty."

I hope you understand I make my own weaves of Lacan's threads. I can't do otherwise. I hope Lacanians will not be overly offended or dismissive, just as I hope I have not offended orthodox readings of *Korach*. I am neither Lacanian nor a literal adherent to religious doctrine but am affected by both. With poetic license, I feel more free to say what is in me to say.

On one level, "You are my woman" affirms "you" and likely "myself" as well. On another, it negates. In one instance, an eager lover recounted how blissful it felt staring into the face of the beloved. He was so filled with feeling, expressive. And she, who seemed eager a moment before, recoiled. His bliss made her paranoid or, better, made her unseen. Suddenly, she was bothered that he saw only his own feelings. His bliss filled his universe. But she was somewhere else, outside it. He did not know where or who she was. He could not find her, could not begin to.

Here the "you" of "You are my woman" was imaginal, a fiction, a signifier triggering his own emotional constellation which he took as real for both of them. Where was the actual bond, the pledge, the trust? In his mind.

Of course there are moments when the other contextualises such a remark and enjoys it. The two enjoying a moment of togetherness, understanding the feeling expressed. In that case, "You are my woman" is not taken as a commandment, a crucifixion (crucifiction), written in stone or nailed to a cross. But often enough such a sense, *you* are *my*— takes the breath of freedom away.

You are mine, my version of you, the you I love and want you to be and I want to be that you for you, your man, yours. Thou shalt have no other gods before thee, especially yourself. The first commandment has wide applications in human psychology.

Such a statement of faith, so full with feeling and meaning, may in certain circumstances, wipe the other out, and oneself out as well. One is tied to unconscious tyranny, demand, run by forces one does not fathom, slivers of which are carved into identity feelings.

Similarly, "You are my analyst" can translate into—you are or better be the analyst I imagine you to be. Not the you of real analysis but the you I can work with because you fit well enough into my delusion of what is possible. You fit into what I can endure. But will you continue to be *my* analyst when you do not fit my unconscious formula. Will you become *an* analyst, neither enslaved by my image or by your own? I live in dread of your scorn of my picture of *you* (scorn as another form of slavery) or your attempt to subjugate *me* to your picture. And if analysis is not mutual tyranny as a form of slavery, what is it?

Psychosis may be one moment when full is empty and empty is full (Lacan, 1993, Chapter Three) One may see people as devils and freeze, feel compelled to run away, throw oneself in front of a subway train because God told you to, attack a devil, weep for the fullness of time and human hopelessness. A particular moment becomes saturated with meaning, heightened truth, no room for editing and considering alternatives. One fails to compare one voice with others, one vision with others. One is caught, frozen, gripped (Eigen, 1986, 2011b, 2014b). Psychotic delusion is hard to let go, loosen its grip. It is fullness of a certain sort, filled with meaning you are stuck with. It does not budge, a kind of psychic cement. To be saturated is to be so stuffed that richness of speech and thought narrows, empties. One freezes in empty fullness. Destructive rigidity exploits potential flow.

By bringing together fullness-emptiness in madness, Lacan illuminates a mad dimension that permeates living, e.g., when I claim you, define you, make you "mine". He amplifies aspects of the madness Freud noted as part of being in love, transference, attachment to a leader. Dimensions in which personality is negated in fullness of feeling that has delusional aspects.

How do relationships survive? I sometimes say that for relationships to work one has to be able to make room for not getting along in order to get along. Making room is precisely what madness cannot do.

The idea of full and empty speech has been around for quite some time. Bergson (1998) wrote of creative and conservative tendencies. Existential and phenomenological writers, e.g., Heidegger, Sartre, Merleau-Ponty, wrote of authentic-inauthentic speech. For Merleau-Ponty (1965) the speaking word connoted creative experience, true to the moment; whereas, the spoken word allied with habit, empty talk. Yet we know from life and psychoanalysis, things are not simple—what is full, what is empty? My love for you may be the most authentic fact of my existence—at least as I experience it now. But in two years we will be divorced and move on. What happened to that most authentic moment?

Lacan tunes in to the inauthentic in the authentic, the reservoir of the unknown simplified by personal drama. Yes, bad faith is in good faith. As Pontius Pilate asks, "What is truth?" We find ourselves in seas of experience, seas of exploration without end, until time runs out. We begin to catch on a little bit the more we are. To learn we are never without hysteria and paranoia opens dimensions beyond them.

I can only imagine the moments of enlightenment Lacan may have experienced on reading Freud's (1911c) Schreber case. Lacan speaks of the transivitism of speech, in which I can be you and you can be me, a sense explored by child psychologists. He gives as an example my feeling that you beat me when I beat you, a sense with wide implications for personal, social and international relationships.

Freud focuses on reversals of pronoun, affect and direction (turning against the self or other). For example, I love you transforms into you hate me or I hate you becomes I hate myself. Affects may turn into each other, opposites reverse, love becomes hate, hate becomes love. Pronouns, too, undergo reversals, I become you and you become me. Attributions of attitudes, traits, actions slide from one to another. I am and am not you. You are and are not me. I love and do not love you. You love and do not love me. Reversible parts of the affect field slip through reversible aspects of pronouns. A hate link may remain constant, but who hates who and how may change.

Language can null, displace, condense, reverse, and fuse tense, affect, attribution, person. As noted, I beat you becomes you beat me and vice versa, depending on the moment. The belief that you beat me may justify me in beating you or, alternatively, justify my being a masochistic victim (your beating me makes me the object of desire).

I can feel that what I do to you is what you do to me, or the opposite. Can we know what is going on with us at any given time? There are many variations. A basic aspect is fluidity in the identity field that language makes possible One can turn the kaleidoscope and study "fixed points" that emerge. By opening possibilities, musings, fertile supposing, psychoanalysis opens worlds.

Digression 3: El Topo

A special negative that is a positive and positive that is a negative. And that is just the gateway, a beginning. While writing this paper, I thought of a movie I saw forty-four years ago, Jodorowski's *El Topo*. What is no becomes yes and yes no. Yes-no operating in invisible ways. Slightly different from the realistic saying that yes and no is part of every experience (akin to Freud asserting life and death drives in every psychic act). Woody Allen says "no" to death. If he could, he would x it out. How many want to kill death. John Donne's: "Death, thou shalt die." Not because the poet slew death but because of a power greater than death. At the end of the Passover Seder we sing a song, "One little goat", in which God, blessed be, kills death. The Godly presence dissolves death.

El Topo is more on the plane of struggle, an enlightenment journey movie. The burden is not on God but on the seeker's skills, heart, will, capacities and ability to go beyond defeat. Perception of the situation one is in and right response is crucial. *El Topo* (translation: the "mole"), the hero, had to meet the masters of the desert who test him, act as barriers on the way. In one scene, he must have a pistol duel with a master who barred the way. They counted off, took x steps away from each other, drew and shot. The desert master got off the first shot, right at El Topo's heart, a direct hit, dead centre. El Topo fell to the ground by the shock of the blow. After a few moments you see him beginning to rise, I think shaking his head a little, with a kind of little smile forming slowly. He stands up pulls out a little metal disc from inside his shirt pocket over his heart and said to the master, "It's not good to be too perfect." Then took his shot, successful, and continued on to his next test.

Taoism speaks of a state in which one is so in life there is no room for death. For El Topo, death coated every experience and life exploded it. *His* life—others died. Did death feed his life through them? Part of psychoanalytic wisdom is how experience is divided up by inner tendencies, which may appear in the world like characters in a play. Part of worldly wisdom, a lived personal *Ecclesiastes*, is that there are moments when a heart-shield can save one's life.

* * *

BRUCE: "I feel like you've been away a long time."

M.E.: "Yes. There's something about you or about the atmosphere that is us that opens dream travel."

BRUCE: "The sessions are dreams. But what about life? Are you alive with me?"

M.E.: "Who is alive with who? An analyst who helped me once long ago says that I'm supposed to help introduce you to yourself."

BRUCE: "An extended introduction, no?"

M.E.: "One that never stops?"

BRUCE: "And after analysis?"

M.E.: "You're rushing? You're pushing me out?"

BRUCE: "I felt pushed out. I know people who have felt pushed out. Not with you. I fear being drawn in, soaked in."

M.E.: "Am I a sponge?"

BRUCE: "No, not a sponge exactly. But something is, something that draws me in."

M.E.: "You're not talking about your own psyche, your unconscious that never says no?"

BRUCE: "I was being clever, jumping the gun."

M.E.: "When you say that I picture a gun shooting bullets endlessly, you and I trying to jump over them."

BRUCE: "That's what I fear. That you and I get away, never get hit, never score a direct hit with each other. We slide away unscathed, unscarred."

M.E.: "You know my quote: The fire that never goes out meets the wound that never heals."

BRUCE: "That's what got me into therapy with you. That's what led me to call. I heard you say that years ago when I was thinking of going into training. I don't want you to let me escape. No yes to a silent getaway."

M.E.: "No, we won't get away. I promise. We won't."

CHAPTER SIX

Shame

PETER: "Why am I ashamed about shame? I've done bad things
I *should* be ashamed of yet something tells me I should be
above it. Does that mean I shouldn't admit to it? Be closed
off? Harden, toughen up? How many times have I heard those
words: toughen up! I'm ashamed of being ashamed. I should
be above it."

My thoughts: There is an image of imperviousness. Nothing should
bother me, get to me. Some kind of commandment: "Thou shalt not be
bothered." Not totally sealed off—just enough to blunt feeling yet not
enough to stop seeing and hearing what is going on. Blunt the pain of
injury but stay keen enough to make calculations.

I think of a moment in my childhood when my father yelled and
threatened to hit me. Up to that moment, when he did that I wept and
sobbed. This time something clicked in me. I won't say clicked off, just
clicked. Was I about seven or eight? Something I didn't expect, I *refused*
to cry. Who refused to cry? Was it *me*? Something in me? Will? Where
did this refusal come from? The hardness my patient spoke of happened in an instant. I vowed I would never again give my father the

satisfaction of bringing me to tears. Much later in life I did cry for him. But never again for being hit or yelled at as a child.

Does this have anything to do with shame? Did my father induce shame and something in me refused it? A steel won't. What did I lose by this moment of growth? Another piece of it was a rising sense that he'll be sorry, somehow I would have revenge. Revenge for the pain, the toughening, the tears not shed? For the loss of power, humiliation, helplessness, or simply for loss. *Loss*. To steel oneself, seal oneself is a no solution "solution".

The term "cut off" doesn't quite get there. It was more a contraction, squeezing tight around pain, holding back one's chest, one's heart acting like anal sphincters squeezing back the tears. A kind of inner squeeze that can go on all life long, tightening psychic arteries. Tightening around a fist of self.

Peter doesn't describe tightening-squeezing but being above, over. Hardening that goes on watching, calculating. He has not lost contact with shame but rises above it, transcends it—partly.

PETER: "I vanish in my shame. It sucks me in. I sink, sometimes slowly, sometimes quickly. Into the shame that covers me as I sink into it. I become less and less visible until I scarcely feel myself. I go into the shame to escape it. Shame becomes a hiding place, a place to disappear. You might wonder how I can be above watching it and disappear in it at the same time. Vanish in it and watch above it. You kind of double, like being twins."

At first I wondered if he was fusing different moments but caught on he was speaking of different parts of the same moment. A kind of double capacity, a paradoxical capacity: to be and not be at the same time. Over and over I reach a point where I deeply feel we are amazing beings. To be above, in, with, through, against, ineffable, down to earth, full, null. So many have marvelled at what we feel or how we watch and diagram ourselves as we disappear … and reappear … and … . What is the many coloured robe if not the colours of being. Affect colours, such as red with shame or rage or lust, white with rage or shame or fright, black with guilt, purple with arrogance, green with envy and jealousy and springtime—existence trying to express, tolerate, exceed itself.

Shame—am—ham—me—sham. Shame affects you through and through, your am-ness. We ham it up and there is no sham-less life.

Does necessary acting, phony-ness, pretence add to shame? We feel we should be totally honest yet deceive in order to survive. Indeed, deceive ourselves to bear ourselves. A valuable life tendency that makes us feel shamed by how we survive.

I'm super-aware of hamming. It's like seeing an inverted movie of yourself through the "wrong" end of a telescope. You can't escape an anal reference when you speak of the depths of shame—seeing yourself through your rear end. Asshole shame. Deadly serious ass-backwards vision making life ashamed of itself. How seriously do you take the deadly shameful act of yourself?

PETER: "I sometimes picture myself a gypsy, singing, playing—the way you see gypsies in movies, playing at being themselves, soulful, expressive. The play of soul, the make believe of music, deadly serious make believe of music. I hear the song, 'Play, gypsy, play.' Where am I in the playing? Close to tears. Welling up. Music plays a truly feeling me torn by longing."

Peter touches a truth, I feel, wells of tears. How true are tears? How true can one be with an aerial self watching a longing self below? Is the watcher outside hamming, outside deception? We speak of "crocodile tears". When I was reading Husserl I saw a transcendental self observe identities coming into being. Where did they come from? Can one be only true? Thoroughly self-deceptive yet feel something true? Sincerity may be a mixture but truth is part of it. Does sincerity mean being humble in face of the fiction of truth and the truth of fiction? Socrates critiqued the sophists who could make anything mean anything. Does sincerity mean catching oneself in the act? Is there a transcendental self that doesn't ham, watching an everyday or psychological self that does? And what about crying from the heart, an outpouring of the soul?

PETER: "I eat my heart from the inside. You eat your heart out but there's always something left. A little more to eat. Shame is part of it, eaten alive by shame. But it's not only shame. I can't find it—a nameless something deeper."

The Bible speaks of eating your children, consuming yourself. What eats us alive? Shame surely is part of it. So is fear. And we speak of being consumed by guilt or rage. Is part of the nameless something self-hate? Self-hate and shame feed each other. Freud wrote of affect turning against the self, the self turning against itself. Earlier in his writings, aggression was associated with a life drive. Later, it became associated with a death drive, a falling apart of personality, a return to lifelessness (Eigen, 1986, 1996). A tendency to build unities and a tendency to undo them. Again, doubleness, one with and against the other.

Where do we go in the world of the nameless? We meet the nameless with handles and ignore the open bottom. We latch onto what we can. Instead of bare namelessness we speak of Jesus scorning the hypocrites or prophets admonitions about fooling ourselves and missing what needs attention. We are not what we should be or can be. Are we ashamed of inadequacy and disability as well as duplicity?

In Judaism there is the theme of trying to put God's name back together, trying to put God back together. Is God ashamed of being in pieces? Is God broken inside us and our job is trying to repair the broken God within? Or for us merely the broken self within? How does God become one? How do we become one? Are we ashamed of not being one and of trying to be one? A double shame? Are we ashamed of doubleness? Shame of brokenness? Again, with Freud, a tendency to unite and a tendency to undo unities. Freud emphasized guilt and anxiety but why not add shame?

Do we feel shame insofar as we are cut off from God? Broken pieces of God seeking to re-unite with our source? Shame for just being a person, a human being? Is there something in us that tells us we should be more than human and dreads being less than human? It is more than enough to try to become a human being or, as prophets say, turn a heart of stone to a heart of flesh. Is the heart of stone our sticking point?

There are times I've seen a dog so filled with a sense of attachment it seemed ashamed of being only a dog, as if it could be more. At such a moment, I've had a sense that the dog felt *it should* be more, a feeling activated by closeness to one who *is* more. Shame attached to comparison, feeling more or less by some inner or outer measure. A dog at the moment I am pointing to seems to ache with a wish to reach another level, as if it could push itself just a bit more and find the level of its master. It almost seems it might push over the line but inevitably falls back, only a dog. Yet the ache of wanting more is ennobling with pathos and touches heart.

PETER: "Sometimes I feel ashamed because I *should* be more than I am. 'I am' is insufficient. Other times less is OK. Just me. What's wrong with that? God has it easy on that score—I fancy him happy being *I am I am*. Maybe that's a good model—being what I am."

Freud saying, "I am my own ideal", is densely packed. On the one hand it attests to undying narcissism, an ever self-celebrating I, an important ingredient of the urge to live. On the other, it points to something I can never live up to, an ideal me I will never be. A paradoxical result is an ever self-persecuting I, a persistent pain point one tries to wash away with idealised feeling as it brings one down. I suspect the latter to be an ingredient in a sense of unworthiness one tries to cleanse. In Biblical imagery, a sense of filthiness, impurity.

One may collapse into a morass, give up, and become defiantly indulgent or oppositional. Many responses in relation to persecutory self-pain are possible. "Evil be my good" represents a kind of oppositional indulgence, perhaps vengeance in face of helplessness in terms of forces one is no match for.

Freud tended to call the religious mania to cleanse oneself of sin an obsessive-compulsive disorder and brought out how widespread it is in secular affairs. Such a deep wish, hope, promise by the prophet: Though your sins be as scarlet, they shall be white as snow.

I am that. I will be that. Is this part of feeling I am Brahma, Yahweh? If I am God will I be free of sin?

PETER: "At a party in college someone was talking about ancient times. Athens? Jerusalem? They made a statement I disagreed with and when I became adamant, the person asked, "How do you know? Were you there?" I frightened myself. For the moment my twentieth century self dropped away and I *was* there. I felt I could be anywhere anytime, everywhere all the time. History was an opening, not a barrier. If you asked me if I were Jesus or Moses, I couldn't say no. I had enough presence to realise I could not say, "I am there now." I was at a party, having a conversation or argument in the twenty-first century. My name, Peter, gave me the shakes. Surely I was not *the* Peter, the rock. But at the moment I could not say I wasn't."

I felt my mind going to pieces. I am me … sh-am-me. I am God not God, God is me not me. What held me in the assault of eternity? Fear of being godlike? Shame of being God? Was I one with all or heading for a breakdown? Was I touching rock bottom?"

Peter describes a kind of uncertainty in face of certainty and, I suspect, his hesitation saves him. Shame triggers grandiosity, grandiosity blots out shame. A feeling of godliness lifts us, a sense of lowliness keeps the balance, an inner seesaw. How to work with capacities, learn to use them as they use us and develop together.

Bion states that he felt ashamed of winning the Distinguished Service Order (DSO) as a nineteen-year-old tank commander in World War One. Possibly, in part, shame of surviving? He graphically depicts deaths of those in his charge. In one case, with guts hanging out, a soldier asks, "Will you write my mum?" his last words. An unfinished movie by Kumar Shahani based on Bion's life and writings depicts scenes of Bion's proud mother treasuring the medal and letter of commendation from his majesty, while Bion as surviving captain looks away, barely able to talk, his few grudging words like shame-filled bullets. In a later scene, the young captain hands out DSO's to everyone at a party (Shahani, 1983).

I wonder if Bion was ashamed when he died. He said he died on August 8th 1918 in the Battle of Amiens and I believe him. Many of us have died in some way in order to stay alive (Eigen, 2007). Are we ashamed of dying? There is a saying, "I died of shame." Mortified. Freud often speaks of narcissistic mortification, humiliation. Are we more ashamed of dying or living?

PETER: "I *am* ashamed. I am going under, vanishing in hole after hole. You can't see me when I'm ashamed. Isn't that what I wish? Not to be seen. To remain unseen exposes one like a flag. A red flag in one's cheeks, one's body turning red. I am a red flag waving and hiding in front of you."

Shame goes deeper than we can trace. A narrative associates it with lowly beginnings: from dust we come, to dust we go. Adam—of the earth. A scene in the script of the Bion movie has "P.A." (Psychoanalyst, grown-up Bion) emerging from mudflats, as if being born from a swamp, for a moment trying to walk on water, almost from the beginning experiencing competing modes of experience. There are hints that Freud associates shame with birth of our upright posture, vision taking the place of scent, above superior to below. Structures of our perceptual world (sky above, earth below; head above, genitals and anus below) get encoded in affective, psychological space (Eigen, 1986, 1993).

Adam and Eve, after eating of the tree of knowledge (K), experience shame and nakedness. Yahweh asks, "Where are you." Adam: "Here I am." Y: Why are you hiding? A: I am naked. Y: How do you know you are naked? A: The woman and I ate of the tree and I know.

An inextricable combination of high and low—ashamed of what is below because of K above, higher-lower loaded with attitudes and judgments, partly opening, partly closing experience. Aristotle's "active reason" (Super-K) leaves us with shame for everything below it. Capacity snobbery: Each capacity above looks down on ones below it. Another possibility is capacity partnership: each appreciating the contributions the others make as well as its own. There is a delusional aspect to "hierarchies".

Psychoanalysis is a vehicle to try to explore capacities. "K" takes so many forms: gut-K, heart-K, flesh-K, head-K. Shame feeds on splits between capacities. There are many ways to feel bad about oneself, who one is and what one does.

An alternative version of a basic scene:

Y: "Where are you, Adam? Why are you hiding?"
A: "I'm ashamed of what I know."
Y: "Who said you know anything? Who told you that you know? Did you discover knowledge yourself?"
A: "Ashamed of naked knowledge, something chasing me, disturbing peace. Did I ever have peace? I can't remember. Chased by a need to know."
Y: "You have discovered a need to know?"
A: "A drive to know, a torment."
Y: "Hell?"
A: "Not just hell. Heavenly hell, hellish heaven."
Y: "I know—you discovered beginning."
A: "Yes, beginning and beginning."

In the script for the Bion movie, P.A. says that when he was being born "it seemed like the end and it was just the beginning."

Prophets call for a new beginning. As if in beginnings we start fresh, no shame, guilt, fear, hate. No blemish.

The Garden of Eden story images a set of psychic states. For example, feeling good, good day, good moment. Life is good, Yahweh feels, surveying his handy-work and handy-words. Then trouble. The story expresses how we feel moving from a good, trouble free, peaceful moment to disturbance. Disturbance arises, whether physical or psychic, backache or thought-ache or heartache. Sometimes other people are hell, sometimes oneself is hell enough. Often hell-heaven in a blender. State after state, state within state. The Bible begins with inherent creativeness. The first word of the first book is "bereshis"—"in the beginning", "beginning". In English the name of the book is translated somewhat stolidly as "Genesis". In the beginning God creates or beginning(s) create God. God creates beginnings. Creativity and beginnings are strongly linked, creative beginnings.

As I sat with Peter, I felt a welling up of love of creativity, creativity love. What happened to shame? Shame of beginnings? Creativity shame? Should I be ashamed of going somewhere else, into my own experience? I remember a moment in my first clinic job when the director of the clinic asked me how I was doing after I was there awhile. I said, "I don't know about the patients, but I'm getting a lot out of it." I felt a kind of creativity in sessions I had never known. The director said, "Well, at least someone is getting something." I stayed there more than ten years.

In Peter's session I felt a kind of prayer forming, an exclamation: "God, what creativity does, what creativity is. It permeates us." I love Winnicott's emphasis on perceptual creativity—the very act of sensing.

Soon enough drama permeates, much as in a Punch and Judy show all is well and then the devil appears. Or in a Laurel and Hardy movie Laurel says, "What a beautiful day", a signal for all hell to break loose. A drama of disturbance in paradise, built into paradise, added to by narrative after narrative.

Is the idea of tabula rasa a wish? Wipe the slate clean, begin like a new born babe. Is there a bit of reality in this wish, fact in this figment? An ever renewing seed?

Disturbance can be like a mosquito or fly bite or serpent poison running through one's psychic system. Paintings of Satan tearing and eating human flesh mirror psychic inflammation. One often lives with chronic disturbance one adapts to, gets used to, more or less—up to a point (Eigen, 1996, 1999).

PETER: "I dreamt of shit coming out my mouth. So much for words. I remember you saying shit in dreams can sometimes be self-hate. Hating myself. Feeling I'm shit. I see it as cement, soul constipation. And now it's coming like vomit, my mouth an ass. I am hoping a dam broke. That there is movement in this movement and I am not merely shitting out my soul. Or perhaps my shit soul is finally coming out—again."

A lot of shit comes out of our mouths. We have all sorts of views we think are right and fight views of others we feel are wrong, viewpoints a source of war or form of war. We are addicted to ourselves, to shit we experience as gold. But there is also the chronic self-hate Peter describes as cement, soul-constipation. Solidified self-hate can be part of a psychotic element in us. It doesn't budge and acts as an alternative psychic centre or anti-centre. Whatever we propose, whatever good comes up, self-hate critiques, blocks it. At times, nothing seems more real than coagulated self-hate and we may do anything to escape it, including kill ourselves or others. We speak about madness of war or familial murder, a blight that stains both inner-outer realities. A blight that is part of our lives, perhaps part of life.

Endless self-hate, endless shame. Shit associated with shame, self as shit. How do we live with it? Many manage to make some room for it, until it blocks too much nourishment and breathing becomes harder. Is Peter cleansing himself, trying to rid himself of something bad, trying to communicate an unsolvable emotional predicament? Discovering or getting rid of himself, discovering a way he gets rid of himself? Is shame a defence against disappearing, both a fight against vanishing and signal from the void? Does our hunger cause shame?

We have many emotions looking for occasions for use. Perhaps a kind of Ur or generic eating oneself inside, sometimes directed at masticating and digesting experience but also the opposite, expelling, eradicating, and something else, more like torment, tormented by various forms of aliveness, tormented by self. An intrinsic torment by life, aliveness, self. We are reproached by our own life.

Is shame a parasite on life or part of life's self-expression? In what ways both?

Shame, guilt and fear have deepened experiencing for me. For one thing, the intensity of these states brings me to places I might not have found otherwise. It's a little like drilling a hole through the earth and coming out somewhere else, another side. Black hole of shame as opening to a deeper sense of self. How is this possible?

It is also possible and important to grow through good feelings and peaceful feelings. But depths of the negative can open pores you didn't know were closed as well as close pores you didn't know were open. Life cuts both ways, works through multiplicity. What seems like contradictions to us are simply ways life works.

We call too little shame inhuman. I once asked two teachers the difference between schizophrenia and psychopathy. A teacher replied, "One is an open wound, the other all scar tissue." Another said, "The psychopath is someone who does not have the common decency to go crazy." One takes colourful answers like that with a grain of salt, but also a grain of truth. How much shame was felt or expressed by Hitler and his ilk over the Holocaust! We speak of guilt deficiency in psychopaths but could also speak of not enough shame. "You should be ashamed of yourself!" words that curse childhood yet have very real application in the social body, where shameless acts of political, economic, military self-aggrandisement can wound whole sectors of a population. On a smaller scale, shameless adult bullying can ruin a home. Recently, we have been treated to shameless, self-righteous acts of public beheadings. We have quite a history of cutting heads off—the guillotine, Judith and Holofernes, head hunters, shrunken heads, heads on swords as part of the swagger of war. Who are we? Where is our mutual shame? Would you behead someone? Does it depend on circumstance? Shouldn't we all be ashamed in front of each other? Wouldn't that temper ill will and violence, foster humility, respect?

On a lesser level, beheading is part of language—to chew someone's head off is to behead another with words. Language tells us there are many ways to lose one's head. Many patients tell therapists details of processes involved in losing one's mind and the struggle to regain it—less a regaining than learning to undergo further births (Eigen, 2014a).

A good politician who lost an election was asked how he feels. His response: "I cut my nerve endings a long time ago or I couldn't be in politics." In his case, affective anaesthesia enabled him to function and try to be helpful, while steeling himself against being wounded. One can easily imagine the reverse, cutting nerve endings so as not to feel the consequences of pain one inflicts on others. I once wrote an online book called *The Age of Psychopathy* (2006b) depicting aspects of this dynamic, mostly in relation to guilt.

There are many ways we cut emotional nerve endings to get along in daily life. Psychoanalysis has many studies of too little or too much emotion, too little or too much self or other centeredness. In some passages, Bion (1994) wrote of narcissism-socialism balance, tendencies that can work for and against us.

Where does shame go during meditation, emptying self of self? Moments of peace. The throbbing beat of self giving us a rest. I easily appreciate a picture of the whole world meditating together, moments beyond war. The prophetic vision of laying down weapons and letting other capacities blossom.

And what about weapons one wields against oneself, inner weapons one may not even know. So much self-harm goes on outside awareness. People say that shame has to do with one's whole being, to be ashamed of oneself. Shame of self can be pretty total. One might say I am ashamed of my body or a part of my body or a particular trait. But ashamed of *my self*, of me, of self. I'm so embarrassed I want to disappear. How can I, dare I, have or be a self at all? Being invisible would not be enough. I would have to not be at all.

A tendency not to be. Freud, partly, encoded this in the "death drive", a falling apart of unities dropping into entropy, a gravitational pull in which organic dissolves once more into inorganic matter—the peace of no consciousness, no animation, the end of pain, effort, and struggle. Death, Freud remarked, is character wearing itself out.

Whatever one calls this, however one understands it, it is very real in the lives of people. Bion describes it as a destructive force that goes on working after it destroys time, space, existence, personality. There are varied visions of such a force. Many try to take the edge off by associating it with re-creation, wiping away the old and emergence of the new, creative destruction. But the force of death can't be wished away. It can take horrible forms, destroying one's being from within, emotional self-destruction. Suicide is one outcome, bad enough, but there are, as we know, harrowing living deaths.

PETER: "I dreamt a door closed. I was locked out of my apartment. All the apartment doors in the hall became blind eyes, black holes, and I began to disappear. I fought to stay alive but it was no use. In a few moments I would be dead. I lay on the floor waiting. Thoughts and feelings became an intravenous drip, dripping into me slower and slower. When they stopped my brain would die and heart stop beating. I felt less scared accepting my fate. I thought there was nothing I could do but there was one thing I could not stop doing—I could experience my own death, at least the start of it, or the middle. I would not be there for the end—and then death came. And kept coming. That was the new beginning, the surprise. There was no end to death. It kept coming in waves, waves of death. And I was there, a body ship afloat in its own death. Death kept beginning. No, that's not right, not quite. Its beginning was lost. All I can say is it kept going.

"I thought it would wipe me out but I feel more real. The realness of death makes me more real. I think of a war movie, soldiers bailing out of a plane over enemy territory, one after another. That's me, bailing out, one me after another, me after me jumping, opening, landing, I'm next in line … the next jump will be me … I will jump into my own reality …

"I was sucked into a black hole of shame and can't stop multiplying."

A few days later:

PETER: "I can't keep up with myself. Before I felt I couldn't move and now can't stop. I felt I was dying and now I'm jumping with life. I'm afraid it's all a crazy illusion. One moment sick of heart, then shocked—dream shock therapy—and I can't stop. I don't know what is happening. Will I come out of this? Will there *be* anything left of me?"

SAINT PAUL: "It is a dreadful thing to fall into the hands of the living God."

And the living psyche where everything becomes everything else and zero and itself.

Taking liberties with a Bible story: God said to Korach, "Be ashamed of yourself." Korach challenged Moses. He argued, "What gave Moses privilege to say what God wants? We are all God's children. What's so special about Moses? We are all special." Some rabbis say Korach was a spokesperson for democracy, others say he spoke from his own arrogance, vying for power in the spirit of a sophist or demagogue. So what happened? A hole opened beneath Korach and his followers and swallowed them. Swallowed with shame? Whose shame? It seems that God often was ashamed of humankind. Rage and shame fuse in acts of disappearance. A flood of shame and rage. A hole of shame or rage. Korach vanished in his own hole, God's hole. The anal hole of shame (Eigen, 1993, 2002). To vanish in one's own asshole, a kind of negative uroborus, snake eating its tail and vanishing through its mouth *vs.* snake vanishing up its own asshole. I suspect in shame it's more the latter and rage more the former. Nevertheless, not all of Korach's sons were killed. Some lived to become poets included in the psalms. Language is made for song and poetry, not only power, lies and daily deception.

Many say shame comes from the outside. People make you feel guilty, shameful. Others make you fearful about yourself your feelings, your doing and being. True enough, but I am also speaking for a more invisible process, shame coming from within, origins and end lost. Of course, in-out combine and we only take them apart mentally. But perhaps, as Freud and Bion suggest, inner has its own trajectory and conditions as well as being conditioned. Freud calls id the true psychic reality and Bion speaks of the rise and fall of emotions as experiences of empty and full.

PETER: "Where did I go to? I can't find myself. I am disappearing in front of my eyes. What do we mean by inner eye? Is seeing inside different from seeing outside?"

Freud (1900a) calls consciousness a sense organ for perceiving psychical qualities. What kind of consciousness? What kind of sense organ? What kind of qualities? Love, hate, truth, falsehood, ambition, and so much more? Filaments of being with no name quiver.

PETER: "All I see with inner eyes disappears. Inner eye disappears. Is it blind? Where does that leave me when I see myself but can't feel myself?

"Shame vanishes like a mouse in an invisible hole. Darkness deeper than shame."

The capacity to feel is an inner "eye", feeling that senses. Milton wrote of profound blindness and Freud blinding oneself so one can see. But how to use it?

When Japanese soldiers in World War Two committed hara-kiri, did this come from outside or inside? A shamed samurai leader committed ritual suicide. A suicidal urge deep in culture. To kill oneself out of shame is one form it takes. What if one resists that pull and waits for a deeper darkness where life ceaselessly re-forms?

Is there such a thing as killing others because one is ashamed not to? If only Hamlet waited and went through the shame of not getting revenge for his father's death and lived the creative darkness he courted, the pregnant darkness that lived *him*. Creative waiting rather than giving in. I have worked with psychotic individuals who felt shame at not following the inner voice's commands which would lead to murder or suicide. Ashamed of living, of saving their existence. They see themselves as cowardly, too weak to follow the Command. And yet this weakness saved them from madness (Eigen, 1986, 2002).

PETER: "I met a girl who seemed to love adventure, a free spirit, ready. She follows aliveness. As I got to know her, I began to wonder if soon it would be my turn to be discarded when aliveness lessened or took another form. Not exactly unexciting but less heightened, maybe more tender, caring. I began getting ready to be dumped. One day words came and I said, 'You need someone to get rid of.' At first, she looked at me as if I were trying to suck the life out of her, denying her right to go where aliveness led. 'Are you trying to make me feel ashamed of myself for being me?' She reproached me, which I took as a need to rationalised her wish to be done with it, to move on. For her, this was the way life works. But the thought stayed with me and turned inward. Do we need someone to get rid of and is this someone oneself? We are good at getting rid of ourselves."

Experts at looking through both ends of a telescope at once. Entering into and getting rid of. Shame doubles into hypervisibility-disappearance. Running towards-away from ourselves is an ancient image, a structure moulding outer-inner worlds.

PETER: "When I was running in the park, I heard a father ask his little girl, 'Can you tell me more about what you remember when you were little?' I was sorry to run past them, tried to linger but my pace carried me on. She couldn't have been more than five and she was talking about what she remembers when she was little. What a beautiful thing to ask one's little daughter, replenishing her own contact with herself. Shame's opposite. They looked happy and full, linking with themselves through the other, with the other through oneself—a model of human behaviour at its best. But I can't help feeling we also need the worst."

"Lord, save us from ourselves. Yet I marvel.

"Everyone was running faster than I. Walkers passed me. I felt I was in reverse, going backwards like you sometimes do in a train. Slower and slower. I felt, this is it, now I will be gone, disappear entirely. To my surprise, another thought unexpectedly lifted me: feeling smaller and smaller enabled me to find my niche in life, my place. I like my little world, my little things. They fit me. I would drown if life were too big and I couldn't be me. Vanishing pleases me. Not being too noticed lets me do what I can. Smaller space gives me more room."

The Talmud says there is nothing worse than shaming another person and associates shaming with death. It also speaks for giving oneself the benefit of the doubt, taking the edge off shaming oneself. Self-shaming is a kind of suicide.

PETER: "I burnt with shame when I criticised my parents yet they deserved it. They should be ashamed."

Shame-fire, where does it come from? I see a deep fire that goes in many directions, shame part of the flame of life, a flame of spirit. Fire is one image. The sound of silence another, a bell with no sound that turns into all bells and whistles and rings one into existence.

PETER: "Let me out of here! Get away from me! I get to a place where I want to tear my way out, push the other away. Let me out— Get Away! I need to breathe. In the hospital I thought, "I am unborn." Now I feel not born enough. Where will I go? I need space.

"It is a shame to go through life unborn. What do I look like? It makes me cry."

I think of wondering aloud whether the woman he spoke of earlier felt like getting rid of him or he felt like getting rid of her. It could be she liked him and he liked her but the need to get rid of smothered liking. The mutual liking which he so treasured in the father and little girl was in danger of being stillborn. Which was stronger, getting rid of or letting in? The life he saw in her was likely his own life too. When he spoke of her need to have someone to get rid of he was, partly, mirroring himself. We speak of a need to find and be or become oneself but we ought not underestimate a need to get rid of oneself (Eigen, 2005).

Trapped within, afraid of intrusion, claustrophobia-agoraphobia of the self. Kafka called his life an incomplete moment. Perhaps one is an experience waiting to be born, a faith aching to give birth.

PETER: "Actually, I prefer being with those who do not feel born. I back off from those who are too born and proud of it, those who glory in self. I feel drowned by too much display of life. Affirmation bullies. A manic yes makes me recoil. I'm more at ease with homeless waiting. I leave when I'm with others. They see me leaving and I feel ashamed that I am thinking bad thoughts about them. It's my fear of life. Response junkies push me around, blow dust off me I need.

"As a child I used to be ashamed of my father's habits and wondered, what did people think? I was proud and ashamed to be with him. Was it my shyness I was ashamed of, locked into myself? His voice was strong, mine weak. I wondered, would mine ever be strong? Yet his loudness shamed me. Shame by association, jails of shame and fear. Shame jails. Are we more ashamed by what is born or not born?

"I see you waiting for me but are you there? Are you invisible to yourself too? Some wonder if the Holocaust ever happened. I wonder if King Solomon's temple was ever there. I thought it was invisible with one visible wall protruding from the Ineffable. Do you feel a temple within or are we all fairy tales? Shame forces us to feel here even if we are mostly invisible. Shame is grounding.

"We are sore thumbs sticking out of existence, throbbing infections we need to quiet. Are you my tranquiliser? It is so hard to be together. Life is an infection that keeps on throbbing. Is there a physician for life? I'm not doing too well, are you?

"I feel ashamed for not destroying myself fully enough. There are groups ashamed for not destroying others fully enough. We will never understand a god of life who can't seem to get enough destruction. I have always felt something right, something wrong. Something deeper than everything that bothers me."

Peter speaks of an opening beyond the self-tormenting self, something deeper. His remark reminded me of another patient who asked, "Is there anything greater than reality?" The real of magic the magic of the real.

Shame is often treated as a second class citizen, more infantile than guilt. Guilt is associated with recognition of harm caused others whereas shame is focused mainly on oneself. There is more other-consciousness in guilt, a need for reparation. Yet shame is often agonisingly other-conscious at the same time it spreads through the self.

I feel less inclined to see shame or guilt as higher or lower but see where each leads and give both their due. There is much to learn by entering fields of experience each offers. Some of these issues were raised on a panel I was on for the Philoctetes Society, 2007, "What is guilt?"

Shame can stimulate a high growth state. It can be characterised by acute awareness, a heightened sense of being or being in jeopardy. It can bring to bear capacities that contribute to the feeling of being me, making me self-aware through heightened self-consciousness. It is also in touch with another's awareness, particularly the other's perception of me, real or imaginary. An acute sense of the other's subjective view of me can grow to encompass realisation of my effect on the other. Shame can act as a conduit to a pressing sense of the realness of mutuality of subjectivity and how we are tied together through our shifting states. A heightened concern with my own reality can evoke awareness of the sensitive centre of the other as well (Eigen, 1993, 2004b, 2011b).

Accidents of language—words in shame: am ham sham, me. Some interpret God as *am*. And for us ego creatures, me-creatures: *Me am*. It did not escape me as a child that my initials are ME, and since my middle name also starts with e, a great big MEE. Did that mean I was simply egocentric? I saw from an early age my father was egocentric.

Outside the family I encountered many self-centred people. This MEE has a big history in the human playground.

It was not hard to move from there to realisation of the role deception plays in life. My father swore concern for others and could not let in his egocentric effects on me. Was concern simply a lie? I don't think so. We are more complicated. To be self or other centred does not preclude the other. We are both and deceive ourselves about the mixtures. Lies are not simply lies and truth not simply truth. They are part of life and like psychic plants have many roots and branches. "Lies" are ways life affirms itself, manifests. As Freud pointed out, there may be truth in delusions and delusions in truth. In lived reality, there are rarely sharp divisions between truth and falsehood, even though something in the human mind has tried to make it so, a kind of simplifying lie in the use of truth.

There are extremes and conditions in which differences between truth and deception seem flagrant but often I think of them as sand-wiches, tangles that bug perception. I suspect this is part of what led Bion to distinguish truth-compassion from truth-cruelty. How we use capacities has an affective quality. In *Coming Through the Whirlwind* (1992), I wrote about a psychologist who nearly ruined his life with his dedication to psychological truth or his version of it, using it to hit flaws he saw in others. He felt it his mission to bring out truths others denied. How true was this destructive use of partial truths? In his case, we were able to pull back from the abyss with real emotional growth.

When my father was in his last months of life he could not believe he did and said some of the things that happened when I was a child. He was appalled by himself, a kind of satori when truth and decep-tion reverse. Shame here represented growth of perception. Something in me softened. In the weeks ahead he asked me to say kaddish at his funeral so as not to shame him. In these near life end conversations, shame acted as an intimate link between parting presences who, what-ever else was true, loved each other deeply. Shame brought us closer and opened a deeper space for love.

Freud and Bion used the word "indistinguishable" to characterise roots of experience that later may emerge as discrete tendencies. The unknown substratum is touched on by many authors: Bohm's (1980) "implicate order", Matte-Blanco's (1975, 1988) "symmetrical uncon-scious", Werner's (1940) "syncretic" mode of experiencing, to name a few. We ought not take for granted that we know what truth and lying are, how they function, where they come from. They may intertwine in many ways, often playing a role in psychic fecundity.

There are passages in the kabbalah that suggest what we call God and Being grow out of a more primordial reality with no concept, name, image, representation. Sometimes it is called That or What or Not, but these attempts are derivative (Eigen, 2012, 2014a, 2014b). Going still further, "it" is called Ein Sof, without bounds, infinite. We go further and further through a kind of intimation, an intuitive ineffable sense of contact with the unknowable. Re-founding (re-finding) our being on this "contact" is deeper than shame and other affect states that play a role in reaching it. Writing such a sentence may look like an attempt to represent the unrepresentable, which reminds me of lines about Tao—if you say it, write it, it's not the Tao.

Bion, who said he used the Kabbalah as a framework for psychoanalysis (Eigen, 2012, 2014a, 2014b), developed a notation for unknown reality (in psychoanalysis, unknown emotional reality): "O". Some make the mistake of equating O with Being. Bion is clear that O remains ineffably unknown and primordial, neither being nor non-being. As in Kabbalah, God as well as being and not-being grow out of unknown reality that O signals. (Bion, 1994, pp. 323, 325; Eigen, 2012). Unknown reality that pervades us, that we are or are part of. What this offers is profound hope for change, development, further experience. Life opens in ways we cannot fathom, mystery without end. One can go further than who or what one is now, a vehicle for unknown possibilities of experience.

PETER: "I feel like everyone and no one. Old as before the world and new as today. All new, partly new, totally here and partly not at all."

Peter has caught a whiff of a primordial state. There are many variations of time-timelessness and qualities of self/no-self feeling. To use Bion's map (1994, pp. 323, 325; Eigen, 2012), many expressive states grow from the primordial unknown.

What are we looking for? What is looking for it? What kind of world do we live in? What kind of world do we create? Where is the flame?

PETER: "When I come out of living forever, back to planet earth, I am confronted by facts that disappeared when I was eternal.

Where will death fall? Who will die next? What kind of desperate war games are we playing with grown up toys. Murder is a game in which we make believe we control death. We have a military core. We are military beings. Rage blots out shame at sacrificing others for one's wishes. It is silly to say war is profitable, death is profitable, murder is profitable. Why not? That this is so shows us something about ourselves, who we are. Who I am. I get off the hook by saying I am a self-killer, playing down what I do to others. Help me, help me are words that come as I fall asleep. Help me not kill myself. Help me not kill and maim others. I can strike you dead with a look. You can kill me with a word. We are killing the waters with our plastic excrement. Soon there will be nothing to breathe. I swear, it is the way I felt as an infant. It is what I lived through, fought through as a child, starving, suffocating."

We mimic control of death because it controls us. Is killing shameless? Was Cain ashamed? He justified himself by grievance, a moment that mirrors how mind can work. Murder as protest against injustice. I feel Cain-like often. Someone gets favoured, I get pushed aside. But murder? Perhaps Cain felt he was murdered and killed in return. What I've learned in our work is that murder happens inside. We kill ourselves with anger, adding self-injury to being injured by others. We need our anger even if we don't know what to do with it and we just can't make it go away.

When I was a child I heard that people who lived in glass houses shouldn't throw stones. Only now, at seventy-nine, I begin to get a fuller sense of this image expressing a tropism to destroy, to injure, to hurt the other at our own expense. A happening permeating psychosocial realities, individual, family, group.

Shame is what the Bible tells us Adam and Eve felt at knowing they were naked after eating the apple. No great crime here. No one murdered, no mass murder. One could say eating the apple was a kind of cannibalism. A spiritual cannibalism precipitating a state described as eating oneself alive, eating one's insides out, partly precipitated by a sense of evil.

I think of a Tom Stoddard play, *Artist Descending a Staircase*, in which two people die, possibly suicides, possibly murdered by aiming too high, misdirection of hopes. Artists keep trying to kill an ineffable fly that eludes them, as if bugged by the drive for art. I can imagine one of these characters flying down a staircase after missing the incorrigible fly. Another character, a blind woman, admirer of artists, threw herself out a window after discovering rueful consequences of error. Killing oneself in pursuit of what one most imagines one loves.

There are many dreams and myths of descent, going down, falling. Jung brought out how they can compensate for being too high. Going from high to low. Winnicott wrote on body illness as a way of grounding oneself, keeping oneself from flying too far away from body and life. The old saying, pride goeth before a fall and ancient Greek emphasis on hubris. What we are touching here are not simply ways of tripping ourselves or the play of accident, both of which work often enough. But something more, a destructive gradient that works with seemingly irresistible force that will is not enough to offset. On the contrary, a kind of unconscious will seems part of the force itself, a destructive will.

PETER: "I see war within groups and between groups. Uncompromising violence. You once told me Winnicott said that democracy is only a tiny bit of the psyche. I feel it in myself. A strict, harsh inner master who threatens punishment and another nature that is indulgent, life loving, enjoys sunlight, sexuality, being myself without a gun at my head. It's easy to get tied in knots and stop breathing."

Maybe catching a fly means to catch oneself flying. I used to fly in dreams in childhood and also go underground in my own private passages. We have a hard time staying on the ground. Gravity keeps us there but something in us tries to burst out above or below. To die catching a fly—that has to be significant. It is a silly way to die, chasing the impossible. When I see what people do to each other and themselves, I think many people die that way, fooling oneself. To be uncompromising is delusional.

PETER: "The inner master I'm talking about is uncompromising. There is more I haven't said, hard—but I feel something from you and will try, although I'm not sure it can be communicated. There is a vile dense ball inside me filled with rot. I am rotting inside. Not like a corpse, not deadness, not stagnant. Something worse. There is something wrong with me. There is an area inside filled with puss. It does not get better. I've waited years and it still is there. I was acutely aware of it since child-hood. When I gave hints to my parents they said I'd outgrow it. It must be fetid but no one smells it but me. No one notices. I am afraid you will play it down too, look past it.

"When I hold a girl's hand I feel relief for a while, but it comes back more intensely. As if goodness heightens it. I was hoping therapy would get rid of it but no sign of that hap-pening. It's something I have to live with, a scar, no a fester-ing wound. A pain eating everything in its path. But that's not it either, because it has a small location, its intensity is sharp, but the place it's in, the middle of my chest, is not large. It is part of feeling hopeless. This infection inside is what I'm most ashamed of. It *is* my shame."

"Shameless people scare me," I said.

PETER: "Don't reassure me. That doesn't work. My parents did the same in their way. It makes it worse. It makes me think you're scared of it, trying to whitewash it."

"It blackwashes you," I said.

PETER: "Yes, but not all of me. I'm not only ashamed, not only an infec-tion. But it *is* what I need help with, one thing I need help with. *Am, ma*—puss. Make it go away but if you try I say you're mak-ing it worse. I get an awful image of sucking a pussy nipple. A putrid nipple."

"If it won't go away, make room for it," I say.

PETER: "A sick baby needs enfolding but won't be held. It's disgusting but I do feel some relief, something giving."

I think of a vagina moulding around a penis, arms enfolding a baby. To hold another in profound embrace, embracing a sick part of one's core. I think of Saint Frances and the leper. It is not simply saying it—it feels core to core. Not brushed aside, bypassed. What is it one gives? For a moment, one's psychic being? A psyche to psyche touch.

PETER: "How long will this last? There *is* a little give."

I would be hard put to say what goes on in therapy. What one senses has no form but does have reality, intensely. One feels inner changes that sometimes have names and sometimes don't. Peter once said he felt sealed off in a tower. The present moment moved from sealed to a bit of opening.

PETER: "I'm afraid of flooding, going through a hole in the ice and drowning."

Drowning in anxiety, dread. I think of the role of floods in mythic imagery and Freud's associating emotional flooding with primal trauma, leaving one fearful of one's own feeling states. Afraid of feeling. Is Peter experiencing a taste of vaginal opening? There are moments I've felt my body as a vagina opening, my heart as vaginal. Lacan (1977) spoke of an unconscious rhythm as pulsations of the slit, opening, closing. So much of therapy has to do with dosage. There are all at once moments, but much depends on a little at a time. Little felt differences that, after a time, mount up to what Bateson (1972) calls news of difference. Little by little shame is included but one goes deeper than shame.

PETER: "I'd hate to think that there's no more to me than what I am. So much about my personality is raw and stillborn, there's got to be more. I want to be a baby that doesn't drown, that breathes. I could sit here the rest of the hour breathing and crying. That's all I want. That's enough."

To breathe and cry, feel insides, intangible movement, let oneself in without rushing or pushing oneself aside. Who can do that? Even a little can be of infinite value.

PETER: "Too much or too little shame. Is it a matter of balance? Shame is part of being human. I'm beginning to feel ashamed of being human again. There's so much humans *should* be ashamed of. We kill to live. Where do we go with this? I'm not going to solve what no one else solved. But what do I do with it in *my* life? What do I do with *my life*? How do I survive being human? Cain carries the mark of the human. I carry the mark of Cain. We kill ourselves to live. Is this the question we are asking inside—how can I live with myself? And if very lucky, live well."

How *do* I live with myself? What is it that keeps opening and closing?

PETER: "Pieces of shit drop from my asshole—shitting shame. I smear myself with faecal shame. I saw an exhibit where an artist used elephant faeces in his art. He linked the Blessed Virgin Mary with the beauty of elephant dung. It was a scandal for some but had a special beauty. I remember the first time I saw dry cow dung on a field and marvelled at its designs. I learned some would use it as fuel, although now it was merely fertiliser. The relief I felt before makes me wonder if what we think is psychic waste is raw material in creative work. What would that look like—shame, guilt, fear as raw material?"

* * *

Bion writes that the Distinguished Service Order he received after the Battle of Cambrai became an eternal badge of shame. How is it that so much of what the world thinks we should be proud of may feel deeply shameful? Bion added that he felt afflicted by the nameless dread of home leave. He seems to say he was ashamed of his fear but the tangle may go deeper. Did shame play a role in spurring his writing?

So much about Brahma and Yahweh seems self-celebrating but oughtn't they feel shame? Does it run through their essence? Does it ever stop or is there a deeper place it does not reach? Since I feel a deeper place it does not reach and they are avatars of me or I of them, then they, too, must go deeper and deeper, depths without end. What mixtures—is this the bottom line?

Ashamed of being a hero because he does not feel he is a hero even if he is one? One is not one's ideal or feel so even if one is? A spore or virus burrows through identity, *is* identity?

I am me—a badge of shame. *I am that I am* from this vantage point begins to sound more than a little bloodcurdling. Self-justificatory, unapologetic, and sending his son to suffer the human—does that correct things? Blood thirsty. Blood curdling.

I heard a story about two rabbis on a train in Italy, discussing a Jewish false messiah who was supposed to bring peace on earth, good will among men. But when he died nothing of the sort occurred and it was clear he was not the long awaited saviour. A priest across the way overheard this conversation and asked why they didn't believe in Jesus? "And what is the human condition as a result of his coming?" they asked. Wars of every sort, within and between individuals and groups.

Often shame is associated with being seen. One hides from being seen, partly hiding from shame. Where is God's shame? Can he be shameless because no one can see him? One may even hide from the fact of being hidden.

I'm ashamed of myself. I suspect this is one of the most powerful phrases in the English language.

A young bride having enjoyed her first night with her husband (first night, literally), surprised at the fullness of her pleasure, was certain everyone who looked at her the next morning could see she was different and *know*. Shame began creeping in through the portal of this imaginary knowledge. Our minds are very creative and often in scarcely knowable ways create scenarios we live together.

Shame can apply to "higher" functions too. There are whose intense emotions take them to God. They may be ashamed they have not gotten to a higher plane through Aristotle's peak, "active reason". There are mystics whose intellect takes them to God. They may be ashamed of their lack of emotive passion (Zalman, 1973).

Was Mr. Hyde more ashamed or frightened of Dr. Jekyll? Did Dr. Jekyll have contempt for Mr. Hyde? Was he growing in Hyde's psychic asshole (Eigen, 1993), a home of shame? And what of the "brownies", voices that dictated the story to Robert Louis Stevenson, his private muse? The "brownies"—neither Hyde, nor Jekyll, nor Stevenson, part of a creative force seeking someone to mediate it, perhaps part of something more. Authors have always had evil, mayhem, meaninglessness among their themes.

PETER: "I have always loved wisdom in my heart. I seek it when caught in whirls. It gives me a reprieve, a place. Shame and guilt and fear and hate and worry may be part of me somewhere else, other places—but this place is special, a touch of peace. Nothing is solved but something is found."

I reverberate with Peter, deeply so. He spoke something I have felt in my heart ever since I can remember. He touched a place many share, perhaps without awareness. Something of lasting value even though we do not last. It uplifts us while we're here, gives solace and more. Ancient Egypt had a concept—*Maat*—that combined justice, good, truth, and love (Tomlin, 1952). A sensed core or ultimate reality. It is a feeling that can be used in a wish-fulfilling way, as Freud suggested. But it also gives us more, a profound sense of who we are. When we feel it we feel something like Bion means by at-onement with oneself, not just oneself but something of endless depth that we share.

There is another kind of use of shame in language, as when we say it's a pity or shame that something happened or didn't happen, a shame I missed out on something important that I needed. Perhaps I feel and am trying to say, it's a shame to miss out on the Maat moment, a dimension in which everything looks, feels and is different.

I sometimes tell people to think, "I can't do anything wrong." Say it over and over, live with it like a mantra. Far from stimulating grandiosity, the opposite often occurs. Humility and assurance grows, shame shrinks, takes up less room, is less gripping and overpowering. It doesn't go away in defeat, but finds its place in the larger whole, tempers but does not obliterate.

I've heard people speak of a mountain of shame that blocks the self. The biggest mountain is oneself. It keeps changing in size, so tiny it's invisible, so big you can't see anything else. One senses through it something deeper, which softens shame's iron grip. A heart of joy, a heart of tears, touched by time, touched by the inexpressible.

CHAPTER SEVEN

My session with André

My first significant awareness of André Green came when he was one of two keynote speakers at the International Psychoanalytical Association (IPA) meeting in London, 1975. The other was Leo Rangell. I had never gone to an IPA meeting and was all open impression. I felt propelled to go because the first psycho-analytic papers I wrote had recently been published by the *International Journal of Psycho-Analysis,* and I wanted to experience the group that had been so welcoming. I did not meet Green at this meeting but met Marion Milner, Masud Khan and Donald Meltzer, continuing contact with them over the coming years, Marion Milner till the end of her life.

There was a lot going on at this meeting I did not quite understand, particularly a buzz about Bion not being accepted as a full member of the Los Angeles psychoanalytic society, in which Rangell was a promi-nent member. Meltzer, especially, seemed exercised by this and did a lot of running around, late in the game, since Bion had moved to Los Angeles in 1968.

Then the curtain went up for the main event. Green spoke about changes in psychoanalysis, plumbing aspects of Winnicott and Bion, his paper dedicated to Winnicott, particularly emphasising changes in theory and practice in relation to borderline dynamics. As I listened, the words formed in my mind, "Psychoanalytic imagination is alive and well." Rangell spoke about the superego and structural theory. I felt deadened.

I met Winnicott in 1968 and, not knowing it then, would meet Bion in 1977, each not long before his death. I began teaching Winnicott in the late 1960's and some years later Bion as well. I taught the paper Green gave at this meeting for many years, and still include it in some courses today. It made my insides sing when he gave it and still does forty years later.

The thrill I felt when he read this paper was shared by Anna Freud as well. She took the microphone after the speakers and for a few moments stood and looked at the audience. The silence for me already felt momentous—Anna Freud, there in front of me, about to speak, eighty years old. The thrill heightened. And what did she say? I don't remember all her words but these stayed with me, one of many psycho-analytic peak moments: "Structural theory, structural theory—we lived a long time without it."

Inside my thirty-nine-year-old frame, climax after climax. Psycho-analytic imagination indeed was alive and well, and she affirmed it! Her response to Green's paper was full, allied with currents of psycho-analytic creativity.

Two years later I would meet with Bion (Eigen & Govrin, 2007) and a year or two after with Green. I also saw Green give a significant paper on affect at the IPA meeting in Jerusalem in 1977, where we met in pass-ing. Our first real meeting was a year or two after Bion in New York. Both gave seminars for the Institute for Psychoanalytic Training and Research (IPTAR), which I attended. I took advantage of their visits by having sessions with them, which I used to the maximum.

By then I had read Green's work in English and felt resonance with aspects of my intuition. As I entered the room for my session, some-thing in me decided to go for broke, let it all hang out. I took a look at him—much to take in—and started accusing him of stealing my work. He must have read me and used my work to stimulate his own, passing it off as his, without crediting me.

Don't ask if I meant it literally. You might want to try to analyse it as fear of resonance, fear of identity loss in symmetrical contact, or any of a number of possibilities, but we gave no explanations. What happened was an important moment in my analytic growth. He sat there with a semi-bemused face, didn't bat an eye, let me go on and when I felt my communication accepted without counter-attack or explanations, I brought up more of my concerns. Eventually the path took me to a recent dream of a woman I was seeing. In the dream she was a beautiful belly dancer in Arabic dress (my unconscious knew Green was from Egypt). There was much erotic appeal but something wrong with her eyes, or so it seemed to me.

By this time, he knew that Bion told me to stop analysis and get married. He observed that I was still seeing analysts, perhaps afraid of trusting myself. Then spoke of my need to spoil the object, needing to find something wrong with the woman to spoil the link. Later I thought, there was reason not to trust my spoiling tendency and good to have input to correct it. At first I tried to dismiss what he said but it grew on me and, coupled with another important therapeutic encounter, I was able to marry the woman in the dream and become a father two or three years later, something I had wanted since a young man. As our time began to end, Green noted that if more time was left, he would ask me about other figures I brought up in dreams and mentioned them in detail. He left me curious, wanting more.

But as I was about to leave he couldn't resist adding, "You know, there is a significant time lapse between my writing in French and English translations." Implying the work I read came out before not after mine. I felt a smile inside, feeling I was with a human being and the words formed, "Here is a real analyst."

It was a one-two punch, my meetings with Bion and Green, much concordance. They converged on a blocked point and helped open the next phase of my life in family life, writing and work. At the moment I write this I am almost as old as Anna Freud when I heard her speak.

The next time Green and I met was when I was program chair for the National Psychological Association for Psychoanalysis (NPAP) and invited him to give a seminar. I can't tell you my anxiety when I realised that the time we scheduled turned out to be when Stephen Mitchell was speaking for another meeting at the same time, a large, national group at which Green was a featured speaker. I thought of rescheduling but Green balked. This was a good time for him. I asked a more experienced person in programming what to do and was told it's not unusual for conflicts to occur with so much going on in New York.

I picked him up after lunch and drove downtown along the river to our meeting. He likes coming to New York, called it a beautiful city, loves art museums. He insisted a building going up was a parking garage and even when I said it was part of a school by the river, he insisted it was a garage (he was wrong, although for moments he had me wondering). There was a slight scent of wine when he spoke and I thought, ah, the French. There could be arrogance, orneriness and beauty. But in my session a decade earlier, a superb analyst who left a deep impression.

As it turned out, we did not have to worry about having enough people. As the talk began, I ran out to get more chairs. He spoke on narcissism-masochism. And when I and a helper returned with chairs, he remarked wryly, almost sweetly, "Ah, you see Dr Eigen's masochism, missing part of the talk when he could let an assistant bring the chairs." In a flash another dimension, a sense of psychoanalytic humour, playfulness, enabling the "serious" to seep more deeply.

I had worried, would he like our group? Would he want to come back? And shortly before we said goodbye, he suggested calling him for more meetings, even smaller groups. He had a good experience. And so did we.

When we parted, I gave him *The Psychotic Core*, my first book, which came out a few years earlier, hoped he'd read it, like it. Funny, the transference. I invested him with years of elder wisdom. Yet he was only eight years older than I. He could not have been a father. He could have been an older brother. But still, he was a psychoanalytic father to me. It is a kind of novel thought for me to begin thinking of him as a brother. A lot of changes in the decade since our first meeting, the growth of family and psychoanalytic families. Even more changes since our last meeting.

Somewhere along the line, he made an offhand remark about the disappearing unconscious. When he spoke for the national meeting, he had a sense of the unconscious vanishing and felt relief for unconscious resonance in our group. I sensed, as I did when I first heard him in 1975, the unconscious alive. Lacan eventually began speaking about the unconscious as "real" (Soler, 2014). Perhaps he, too, felt strong social-psychological forces engaged in destructive attempts to wish the unconscious away, partly allied with what I called "sanitised sanity" (Eigen, 1986, 1999).

What was it about Green's 1975 talk and paper that so intrigued me? It felt a bit like a psychoanalytic credo. For one thing, he put madness centre stage in psychic life. As Henry Elkin once said in a lecture, "Behind every neurosis is a hidden psychosis." Instead of (or in addition to) neurotic symptoms expressing perverse dynamics, both perverse and neurotic states were attempts to deal with aspects of madness. Green was, in part, summarising a thread of psychoanalysis present in M. Klein, Winnicott, Bion, and others, where psychosis was acknowledged as a complex force in human existence and not an unusual aberration. Psychosis was coming out of the psychoanalytic closet.

In *The Psychotic Core* (1986) I brought out how central it was in Freud's work as well, although often in implicit ways. The structures Freud elaborated later in his life had roots in aspects of psychotic phenomenology. The id a seething cauldron of excitations where the law of contradiction does not hold, the early ego an hallucinatory organ developing anti-hallucinatory aspects over time, the superego prone to overdoing it, persecuting personality. In various texts, Freud wrote of mad aspects of love, identification with parents and leaders, transference phenomena, and what seemed like inescapable war.

Green's sensibility moves towards focus on madness through text-analysis and clinical realities. In the sketch that follows, I've taken some liberties, rewriting, rephrasing, adding aspects of my own associations. In particular, Green focuses on borderline dynamics, naming four defences or ways of expressing a double root of madness, a central double anxiety: intrusion-abandonment anxiety. Green writes intrusion-separation anxiety, which I've changed to abandonment in order to bring out the extremity of feeling involved, what Winnicott (1974) and Elkin (1972) called basic or primitive agonies.

Too much of the wrong thing, too little of the right, fused and alternating. One thinks, too, of the schizoid personality, propelled towards and away from contact at the same time, moving in one extreme or another depending on the dominant fear-need ratio. Bion spoke of maximum-minimum emotional states, and here we have both combined to the maximum and minimum at the same time (Eigen, 1998).

The four defences in face of central intrusion-abandonment anxiety (dread) involve: 1) somatic exclusion, where psyche is jettisoned in the body, what we often call acting-in; 2) acting out; 3) splitting (Melanie Klein attributed loss of affect to proliferation of splitting, affect diffusion); and 4) perhaps the most devastating of all, decathexis, energy turned away from the self, perhaps even from the whole of personality and being. Here the hole in "whole" becomes more than hole, more than loss and depletion, although those may be included. From one angle, it represents stages along a gradient of negative narcissism and death drive, death-work, but even that may be too constituted, too differentiated. There are cancers that work by loss or breakdown of structure, becoming less and less differentiated. But even that is too much of a figure.

A basic clinical problem that exercised Winnicott was depersonalisation, feeling unreal to oneself, an important theme for Klein and Bion as well. Winnicott sought to find and portray conditions that personalise existence, in which a sense of feeling real grows. Green was a deep reader of Winnicott and Bion as well as Freud. He studied with Lacan and absorbed much but was one of the few in French psychoanalysis that also found roots outside, especially British.

The importance of Green's writings on decathexis can hardly be overestimated. It has confluence with Bion's (1965, p. 101; Eigen, 1998, 2011b) destructive force that goes on working after destroying time, space, existence, personality. You might say it is beyond loss insofar as it takes the air out of existence, the existence out of existence. We are left with a nosology of nothingness.

Freud wrote that in psychosis libido is withdrawn from the object and over-invested in the ego, the famous "megalomania" dimension. Green goes farther, suggesting libido is withdrawn from the ego, from the self, from one's being. One is left with zero. No-mind, no-self, no-life. A domain opens that is not just ego and/or object cathexis but no cathexis at all. For some, a state from which there is no return.

Much of the rest of the paper will spiral around facets of nothingness, not necessarily as Green might always like, but "nothing" has a long cultural and psychoanalytic history and much to offer.

Federn (1926; Eigen, 1986) noted that ego boundaries keep shifting, more inclusive, less inclusive. Boundaries can vary like barometric pressure from moment to moment, or freeze in more or less rigid organisations. Using Green, one might go even farther and depict the ego as excluding itself, in effect, getting rid of its sense of realness.

Of course, even in psychosis one can't stay at zero. Thoughts, images, hallucinations flicker on and off, with greater or less persistence, often loaded with terror, nameless dread looking for a local habitation and a name. Even nothing can be loaded with affect. Nothing can have affective nuances and densities.

One might conceive of many states of nothing rather than a single state, multiplicity of dimensions and possibilities. For example Marion Milner (1987; Eigen, 1983, 1993) writes of creative emptiness and nothingness as part of openness. Bion (Eigen, 1996) distinguishes between states of nothing that close and open growth of experience. Moncayo (2012) links Lacan's empty subject with Zen emptiness and Kabbalah infinity (Ein Sof, infinite beyond boundaries, concepts, images).

On the other hand, there is devastating nothing, associated with loss of life and possibility, the negation of pleromatic birth, potential without beginning or end. In Green's (2011) last book, published just before his death, he focuses on "failed" cases, as if needing to confess and explore psychoanalytic limits. Dynamics around nothing can be very complicated. Some cases may fail for not being able to let go of "something", something deformed, poisonous, "secure", rigid—a kind of overly zealous self-preservation taking a wrong turn in face of fragility. In some instances, a wrong kind of something in defence against nothing.

Green distinguishes chaos from nothing. I once heard him say, "Nothing is not chaos." I think of the terms "formless and void" in Genesis, for which there are many interpretations. For some, formless is associated with chaos and void with emptiness (a Hindu saying associates everyday life with the past, dream life with present, and dreamless void the future). Loss of form and movement towards chaos is associated with entropy, and for Freud, the breaking up of form with the death drive. There may be a double directionality in the death drive, towards chaos (entropic loss of form) and towards nothingness. Both tendencies involve destructive and/or creative processes, depending on function in a given context.

The story in Genesis distinguishes and links the two in processes of creation. God trembling over the waters, the abyss, the deep, chaos/formless and void/nothing. Chassidus (Schneerson, 1998) speaks of God creating the world every moment out of nothing. In this vision, *you* are being created every moment out of nothing, always a chance for further development, deepening. Chaos, the deep waters, the abyss, formlessness, void are parts of the raw material of creation, primeval creative "instruments".

Winnicott emphasised creative aspects of dipping into chaos, states of unintegration rather than disintegration, the latter more associated with annihilation, the former with potential. In one case (1953), he emphasised the importance of the caretaker being able to tolerate a child's dropping out of life for a time, not always having to be "on" in order to make the parent feel alive. There are many gradations of not being there. Ehrenzweig (1971) spoke of the "vague stare of the artist", a kind of semi-blank state in which perception can reshape itself and develop further.

In parallel fashion, Bion's (Eigen, 2014) grid can depict growth or destruction of experience, a kind of positive and negative grid, experience building on itself and/or undoing itself. Some depict the death drive as active destruction aimed against the self or simply a more passive falling apart of personality, self, loss of organisation. Freud appealed to an image of catabolic-anabolic processes, although he brought out various nuances with other images (Eigen, 1996). Perhaps one can envision positive and negative decathexis.

In his work on autism, Meltzer (1975) wrote of "gone" states, which he associated with the "dismantling of attention". The autistic child could go limp, turn to butter, and lose form and organisation under threat of loss. Where was the child when he seemed to be "gone"? While in autism "gone" may play a role in chronic insulation against pain, experience teaches me that some form of "gone" is important in relationships. It is important to tolerate not being together in order to be together.

One psychoanalytic vision that emerges is a creative function of life and death drives working together, incessantly building up—falling apart, reconstituting, regenerating, regrouping. The two together keeping personality from stagnation. On the other hand, something can misfire, with destruction getting the upper hand, the person going under. Green's depiction of negative emptying out of personality and being is a devastating portrayal of "gone".

Winnicott hints of a positive "gone", a kind of dropping out of life for a time, a vacation from oneself. Having to be a self all the time can be burdensome. One feels relief to feel free from the tyranny of self and even existence for awhile and breathe easier. The *Heart Sutra* in Mahayana Buddhism suggests that anywhere we find ourselves, we can go beyond it. If Chassidus tells us we are created anew every moment, Buddhism urges us to go beyond the state of the moment.

One final word on linking. In decathexis, links to life, self, others vanish. I suspect in our session Green sensed a background danger of loss of linking beneath my spoiling tendency. My attacks on links could create or open a hole through which the wish, need, desire to link might vanish. Freud (1920g) wrote of a loss of energy in the psychic system related to the death drive. In subtle, nuanced fashion, Green affirmed a linking function, my being's movement towards a woman, a growing attachment, a real possibility. Ferenczi (Eigen, 1996), in related fashion, wrote of the mother supporting the child's life feeling in face of the death drive's undertow. Green, so to speak, "attacked" my attacking the image of a woman that would result in one more scuttled relationship, one more move towards zero, one more emptying out that left me nowhere.

He supported life and the other in face of my attacks on it. It could be out of a page of Melanie Klein, but when he said the word "spoiling" it set off ripples. Spoiling the object—and where would that leave me? Alone, without the family I always hoped for. In face of emptying life of life, he supported life, allowing it to build on itself. Freud (1918b) spoke of a "breakthrough to the woman", when noting the Wolf Man's link to a nurse in a sanatorium, a moment the "caul" that surrounded him psychically, a kind of chronic decathexis, lifted. The lift that Green gave me played a helping role through many crises in years to come. There are moments in therapy that help one all lifelong.

CHAPTER EIGHT

Figments, facts, interruption, hints, and …

I think it was in the 1970s that I first saw James S. Grotstein speak in New York City. I felt here was a man I could listen to again and again. I tried to attend whenever he gave a New York talk and when I became program chair for the National Psychological Association for Psychoanalysis, he was one of my first invited speakers. I took advantage of my post by inviting people I most wanted to hear. We were also on a panel of the first international relational psychoanalytic congress, invited to speak on the "relational unconscious" by Adrienne Harris (Eigen, 2004a, 2014b). His wife, Susan, told me after the meeting, "You two make a good team." He could be funny and profound, at the same time searching boundaries at the centre.

Something I got from the very first talk I heard stayed with me all these years. Grotstein (2000, 2007) spoke about the id having to be protected from the ego. Loosely speaking, more broadly, the unconscious needing protection from consciousness. Unconscious processes that include a background subject that supports and/or fails to support the growing personality (Eigen, 1996, 2009, 2011b). Jung already had passages on the ego's exploitation or use of unconscious work in the creation of art, poetry, philosophy, and I would add, depth psychology. Exploitation of psychic depths for the creation of "products", wondrous and nourishing as the latter may be, Taj Mahals of the psyche. Winnicott (1971) pointed out the danger of equating process with products. For example, transitional experiencing goes on and keeps developing long after the teddy is abandoned. Jung, too, contrasted profound individuation processes from mere pilfering the depths.

Bion underlined a positive function of pillaging. One image is the drilling deep below the surface of the brave and driven robbers of the death pit of Ur (Bion, 1994). The robbers accurately pierced surface rock and dirt to open a passage into the Queen's burial area with its riches. Bion sees this as growth of a scientific frame of mind, even scientific greed. The thieves were undeterred by what must have been strong fears of the dead, desecration, revenge of the departed. They braved the unknown and taboos. In laconic fashion, Bion suggests a monument should be erected in their honour, a kind of model in face of the forbidden and its terrors. In this context, he found positive value in greed prevailing over fear, distinct from situations in which the reverse might hold.

I remember in grammar school teachers celebrating Columbus and other explorers for sailing on in face of the possibility that the world was flat and falling off the end of the world for the sake of opening new possibilities. Bion brings out the function of grave robbers in this endeavour. I wonder if this is something that entered Freud's mind, as he wrote late at night amidst his collection of antiquities. Such a range of identifications—conquistador, spiritual leaders (Moses), and those who brought hidden treasures to light, linked with growth of knowledge and appreciation of an almost lost past. Common language links hungry greed for wealth and knowledge and both with power. In the current milieu, I hear statements justifying the very wealthy as knowing how to make money, create wealth, a conjunction of wealth, know-how, ambition, and greed. I would add, luck and circumstance, but I don't want to diminish the strength of association between knowledge-wealth-power, which may be reaching a point where benefits and harms are becoming indistinguishable.

There are, too, situations in which knowledge and wealth are opposed. The happy man pictured in his study, appreciating the harvest of minds through the ages: "My mind to me a kingdom is" (Sir Edward Dyer). Machiavelli said his happiest moments were in his study with his books reading the ancients. And on a related plane, Isaac Bashevis Singer wrote something like: "We are all, even an idiot, millionaires in emotions." In Singer's day, a million seemed like a lot of money. As a youngster I gasped at the awesome salary of $100,000 Joe DiMaggio received. More recently, the head of a school I know told his son, who became a millionaire, "One million isn't very much these days ...", more should be forthcoming.

Heidegger writes of truth—*aletheia*—as appearing in a clearing of being, a disclosure, an opening, very different from the pillaging image, another state or feeling. An opening to a clearing in being, a revealing. Bion (1994) wrote of a selected fact (Poincare) gelling a sense of fragments into a whole, but also emphasised the importance of going beyond the whole, returning over and over to a fragmentary state waiting on further movement. The two positions fragments ↔ wholes are interactively ongoing, contributing to developmental processes, whether growth of experience and/or growth of knowledge. One might speak of a suspicion of "wholes", the danger of being trapped by a mental product as if it were *the* whole, at the same time valuing and working with what mind produces. In an unfinished Bion movie (see below), the priest says, "Sometimes there is nothing to do but wait." At times, patient waiting on O, unknown reality pressing towards experience, the beast slouching towards Bethlehem, a thought, intuition, feeling, sensation searching for a thinker, intimation, feeler, sensor.

Bion has many models. Pillage in one state, opening to the unknowable is another, the first involving greed, the second a modicum of sincerity. Perhaps akin to selfish love on the one hand and love beyond grasp and graspingness on the other, e.g., Spinoza's *amor dei* or the biblical love of the unknown-unknowable, ineffable, infinite God with all one's heart and soul and might and mind. Many currents blend and feed each other, including science, poetry, art, and spirituality. Dramas of generative-destructive threads, entwined in a seemingly endless plethora of ways, ran through them (Bion, 1994; Eigen, 2012, 2014a, 2014b, 2014c).

A symbiotic relation between different capacities is different from a pillaging model: interweaving rather than plunder. But many relations are possible, e.g., positive-negative symbiosis (nourishing or depleting), oppositional (states opposed to each other), multi-ocular mixes (different views fused into a rich field of existence). Capacities we evaluate negatively can have positive areas of operation and vice versa, depending on context and function.

I tend to look at biblical dramas in terms of states of being and psychic tendencies. For example, the creation myth. A sense of something coming out of nothing can be part of many moments of experience. A sense of aliveness growing out of feeling vacant, dead or empty. Eternal moments moving from deadness, tomb, to inner sun rising, self coming back to life, resurrection through black winter, aliveness returning (another meaning of the "return of the same" with "news of difference"). Such emotive shifts occur in many ways throughout a day and lifetime. Dying out ↔ coming back, life ebbing and arising. Emotional shifts are colours on life's palette (Eigen, 2004b).

While one can feel the rise and fall of feeling in terms of loss and rebirth of emotional life, the sequence can be even more dramatic. Rabbi Menachem Schneerson (1998) posits the creation of personality and being each moment out of nothing, here, now, always. This is a radical dramatisation of off-on fluctuations of emotional states.

An ancient and important binary used to organise inner experience is good and evil. This has its important uses but has also obscured possibilities of experience. Embryonic nuances of emotional life seeking birth and growth are often ground up by the good-evil binary machine. There is much to be gotten with a shift of attitude, appreciating nuances of feeling and affective attitudes in their own right.

Over and over in the Bible and life, destruction happens. Melanie Klein writes of good and bad internal objects, internal attacks as well as external. Attacks that come from inside, not only outside. Attacks can show up as part of life myriad ways. We are self-attacking as well as other-attacking beings. Freud (Freud, 1911c; Eigen, 1986) suggested that reversals can happen in terms of affect, object and subject. Love can mask or turn into hate and vice versa. I may feel you hate me when you love me or love me when you hate me. I am and am not you, you are and are not me. I am and am not me, you are and are not you. We can feel each other's identities, up to a point, and exchange or resist them for a time.

Swarms of destructiveness in the bible, whatever else they may mean, express destructive urges in us. Sometimes they give us energy, make us strong. Often they undermine us, fill us with self-doubt and denigration. With shame and guilt and self-hate we eat ourselves alive. Not only attack ourselves, pulverise and damage ourselves. It is not just that the id needs protection from consciousness, it also needs protection from itself, its own self-damaging tendencies, which can be very strong.

Our entire psyche needs to learn to work with itself, live with itself in less self-damaging ways. I take this as an evolutionary challenge, a task.

Not only are the psalms flooded with swarms of destructive realities and feelings, there are high and low emotional moments in changing keys. Many moments the psalmist dies out and comes back to life. The psalms document affect dramas. "Awake my soul, awake lyre and harp, I will awaken the dawn." (Psalm 57) The soul sings, is music. The glory of God and life shines. In other moods or circumstances one feels estranged from existence, alone, "abandoned in darkness". "I have borne sudden terrors, which have become part of me." "Your frightening attacks have cut me off." (Psalm 88; Eigen, 2012). God is the attacker but as a contemporary psychologist, I must also say that the attacker comes from within one's being, one's personality, oneself. My inner Melanie Klein might say, I am estranged from my good internal object, cut by the bad.

Winnicott (1974) and Elkin (1958, 1972; Eigen, 2004b) do not speak merely of good and bad, but dire agonies, hellish torments, and dreads. Bion (1970) writes of catastrophic realities within, even aspects of the birth of self as catastrophic, so much so that a sense of catastrophe can link personality together. The problem has been with us as long as we have had minds. Ancient men drilled holes in skulls to try to let the bad thing out. I've heard, along a similar vein, that ancient Egyptians could pull a brain out through the nose or eyes. So many ways of conveying a sense of a bad feeling within we try to get rid of or ameliorate. One way is to try to attack the pain itself, and when it comes to internal mechanisms this means actually destroying mental functions. One destroys parts of oneself to rid oneself of pain. In one talk I remember James Grotstein imagining an infant internally destroying its developing corpus callosum to cut the link between hemispheres that allow the pain of meaning to develop. I've seen an injured rat chew a painful limb off. How much more difficult with painful minds that are intangible, invisible, ineffable.

The unfinished movie, "A memoir of the future", is based on Wilfred R. Bion's autobiographical works, particularly *A Memoir of the Future*, which was a fictional portrayal of psychoanalytic experience, a dream of psychoanalysis, a psychoanalytic dream. After a decade in Los Angeles, Bion was invited to come to India for a documentary interview in the land in which he lived his first eight years. At the age of eight, as was a custom, he was shipped to England to boarding school and never returned. In his early eighties, on his way to India, he died in England a few months after his arrival. The documentary was never made. Instead, it was decided to create a fresh work drawn from Bion's works. Udayan Patel was an impetus for this and his friend, Kumar Shahani, was the director. They linked up with Martha Harris and Donald Meltzer in England, who supported the project. Meg Harris Williams worked with Kumar Shahani on the script. Scenes were shot in 1983 in India but the movie was never finished, partly because of financial difficulties, partly because of tragedy. For current purposes, I will be drawing from the script as well as movie. The script is in process of being prepared for publication by its authors and I am using it with permission.

The script begins with an un-shot scene framed at the beginning by a pregnant girl in the cellar who, at the end, is led by soldiers to an ambulance with tiger stripes, followed by a quote from the Vedas on the power of the belly. The pregnant girl appears on and off throughout the movie, usually a servant, but also prospective bride, great mother, at once servant, daughter, bride, and goddess. Reversal is an important happening in Bion's sense of the psyche, and in the movie the servant becomes the mistress and reverse. She is called Kathleen and gradually takes on power for me, expressing the fact that throughout our lives we are pregnant with our lives, pregnant with unborn selves and psychic babies, including thoughts, feelings, attitudes, modes of experiencing. A pregnancy that never stops, no matter how many births. Ever ongoing gestation and birth of experience. Gestation that never ends. The real question is can it begin, to what extent, with what quality?

There is much to be said about the tiger theme in the movie and script but I will leave that for another time. Many scenes in the script were not shot. It is impossible to know what would have been added or changed. The actors, too, add unpremeditated moments in the actual filming. At this point, I would like to say more about the first scene.

Immediately following the pregnant girl in the cellar (basement, foundation), a character called P.A. tries to come out of the mud-flats. P.A. (psychoanalyst) is grown-up Bion in his profession. In the movie and script we witness Bion's birth, dramas as a little boy, as a child and adolescent in boarding school, a tank captain in World War One, somites in the womb conversing with the mother. There is fluidity of time, place, and person with underlying faithfulness to emotional reality. Various strata of the psyche intermingle in shifting configurations.

In this early scene P.A. keeps trying to come out of the mudflats. One moment he tries to walk on water, but sludges along. Priest complains about the hopelessness of communication. When he tries to talk something over with P.A., street urchins interrupt him. Priest and P.A. form a duo among other "twins" throughout the movie. P.A. picks up on street urchins and says:

"Street urchins? Who—the somites? The phenomena—the facts?"

A voice, origin of which is unclear—Priest, P.A.'s thoughts, Scientist, other?:

"These ... these ... fictions, figments of imagination, these disguised facts ..."

Scientist gives P.A. a hand to get out of the mudflats. Scientist, Priest and P.A.—a cultural trio. Someone (probably Scientist, unmistakably looking like Einstein) says:

> "Anyone with any senses knows that figments of the imagination are the hereditary rulers of our life. Everything starts as a figment of imagination—a whole structure in itself: its laws of reproduction are its own. Yet, do we hear the body when it wants to tell us something that we do not want to hear?"

P.A. continues slushing along, as we see microscopic events in the water.

The scene is not quite over. P.A. is greeted by Ayah (his childhood caretaker, not seen after leaving India at age eight) who tells him how grown-up he looks, while P.A. voices pain of existence. More happens but we must leave that for other times. What do we have so far? Already an image of a multi-storied psychic building. Not just a finished building that we live in, but psyche growing, building as it lives. Like Adam arising from earth, we have culture arising from mudflats. Priest, Psychoanalyst, Scientist. Since Scientist lends P.A. a hand, one might assume that he was on dry land. It is kind of funny, P.A. wanting to walk on water but moving through sludge. We try to be above it all, above the psyche. Does this mean we try to be above life? Life tells another tale.

One might call the mudflats womb or link it with swamp life. A kind of image of P.A. emerging from a cultural womb filled with dense nutrients. There was a time when people tried to denude mudflats of their rich deposits, dredging, trying to clean them out, repelled by anal associations, useless waste products. As time went on, mudflats were appreciated as a refuge for birds and other wildlife, a breeding ground and hiking through them even became a sport. Now, at least in some sectors, they are preserved and well regarded for a plethora of microscopic and macroscopic life. What seemed so poor turns out to be rich in abundance, life's swarming.

In the script and movie, birth plays an important role, many kinds of birth, literal childbirth but also birth of ideas, feelings, and experience. Here, also, birth of psychoanalysis, psychoanalytic birth. Midwifed by science, but also (mainly?) literature and art and, in Bion's case, music as well. Birth and the possibility—the reality—of not being born.

When Samuel Beckett ended his analytic work with Bion at Tavistock in the 1930s, Bion took him to a lecture by Jung, in which Jung spoke of a woman patient who was never born. This struck Beckett to the quick, a theme he nurtured in his work. In Beckett one finds birth of work about not being born, a theme with wide resonance. Franz Kafka felt his life an incomplete moment. A birth that never fully happened although he tasted many kinds of births and in his writing, creative births. Yet, in some way, not the birth of *life*. He wrote of a door he was supposed to go through that was locked when he got there, failure to be born.

Mudflats remind me of images of a primordial swamp which contains a plethora of life commingled with what to us looks like detritus, putrid with nutriment. We are repelled by its odour and texture but fascinated. Since a child who grew with woods but fearful of swamps, I nevertheless associated birth of life with the density, darkness and muck that scared me and made me feel defenceless. Woods I could explore but swamp was something I tried to get out of, as P.A. did here. It takes much living to value it as part of our fundament.

What does it take to be born? And is part of being born growth of awareness of necessary failure or limitation of birth processes?

Priest already announces an interruption near the beginning of the mudflat scene. I feel like capitalising "I" and writing Interruption and making Interruption a character in the play too, as it is in life. It plays an important role throughout the script and movie. Gestalt psychology studied incomplete or interrupted tasks and tension they create for completion, a need for completion. Many write of need for wholeness, so much so that a counter-movement developed valuing fragments. Life interrupted, caesura, life continuing. When I was in graduate school there was much talk about continuity-discontinuity and creative gaps.

And what about free association and free-floating attention? A need for life between the cracks. Part of why I like this fragmented movie and script, bits and pieces of psyche speaking.

And what is the Interruption that bothers Priest, that makes communication hopeless? Rowdy street urchins. A pattern (Eigen, 1986) I have often found in dreams of people who seek therapy for psychosis in the first years out of hospital begins with butchered body parts in wasteland, often a desert, usually parts of animals. In a year or two, dreams of human corpses coming to life, with creaky limbs and difficulty moving. A year or two later, delinquent youngsters, often teens, scaring the dreamer. The dreamer fears injury—they will attack him or he perceives threats of attack. All three types of dreams are recurrent. It is not difficult to imagine them as different psychic states. In the third type, the dreamer fears aggression aimed at him. In the first two, destruction has already occurred. He does not have to undergo it in the present. Psyche images what happened to it. In the second dream, the dreamer fears coming life, its difficulties and risks, and to see a corpse move is simply scary. But it does not take long to realise that it is oneself who has been dead and coming to life. To come to life is to risk trauma that led to psychic death in the first place (Eigen, 1998, 2001b, 2005).

Aggression that damaged the psyche is pictured outside one, coming at one as the feared delinquents. Perhaps once it came from those who took care of him. At the same time, the delinquents (rowdy street urchins) also depict one's own aggression turned against the self. A self-damaging movement of a distressed and helpless psyche in need of inner resources. My patient is long since gone from his parents' house but not his own. He may be retreating from or fighting a battle of the past, but the turn against the self is ongoing now and must be faced on new terms. In a very real sense, aggression that harmed him may yet help him, if he can find it, make it his own and work with it. The rowdy street urchins are, in their way, alive, part of life outside the establishment, although we now know that criminal elements of society are counterparts of and feed the system. Still, delinquent aspects of self express some need to be outside the system, no matter how much they also may envy and want to be part of it.

Cultural realities and stereotypes play an important role in our dreams. Dickens street urchins—reality and stereotype. D. H. Lawrence's passionate lovers likewise. *A Memoir of the Future* is filled with fusions and juxtapositions of social realities and stereotypes and their reversals, e.g., submissive servants become dominant and prove more vital than newly submissive gentry. Dominance-submission appears as an enduring psychosocial link requiring attention, while particular roles may reverse.

There are "twins", counterparts and their reversals. Two such reversals in the movie and script, written by Kumar Shahani and Meg Harris Williams, involve the Ayah and Rhoda Bion and Kathleen and Mrs. Rhodes. Ayah was Wilfred's caretaker in India for his first eight years and Rhoda his birth mother, the mistress of the house. As the movie went on, the Ayah became more and more dominant, Rhoda submissive. In one scene we see Ayah on a throne. Einstein kisses her hand and Man (or Lucifer and sometimes Saint Peter) kisses her feet. As she assumes vital dominance, Ayah remarks that all the servants are upside down and that she is the most powerful god of all. I'm reminded of stories of Greek gods in which vicissitudes of vitality shift from one to another. Who's got the power now? Which sector of psyche and society, which tendency, how and for how long?

Mrs. Rhodes was young Wilfred's "foster mother" in England, where he was sent to boarding school at age eight. He did not see his mother for three years after the drop-off and never returned to India. Kathleen, the pregnant girl in the basement at the script's start (not shot), and who remained pregnant throughout the script and movie, was at once Mrs. Rhodes daughter and servant, walking through the movie multiple times carrying a tray and serving drinks.

As the movie went on, Fred Bion, Wilfred's father, Rhoda's husband, announced he was going to marry Kathleen who, against Mrs. Rhodes advice, agreed. "I have my hooks in his eyes", she said and the couple walked off.

In the script, a counter scene (not shot) occurs between Kathleen and Mrs. Rhodes alone. Kathleen established dominance and Mrs. Rhodes asks, "Who are you?" Kathleen replies, "I am your maid." Mrs. Rhodes continues questioning and elicits a further response: "A servant … a daughter. Even a mother. Bone of your bone, flesh of your flesh." Not satisfied, Mrs. Rhodes demands or pleads, "Show me truly who you are." Kathleen holds back, "No, you will deny me." Mrs. Rhodes: "Show me." Kathleen warns there is cost to know and Mrs. Rhodes says she can pay. One senses emotional cost, such as that involved in eating the apple. Kathleen decides to reveal herself as the great goddess she is:

KATHLEEN: "I sent you artists, but you did not see; I sent you prophets but you did not listen."

MRS. RHODES: "Open my ears."

KATHLEEN: "I sent you Bach."

MRS. RHODES: "Send me a better one."

KATHLEEN: "I sent you poets ..."

MRS. RHODES: admits these are great men but she is not satisfied: "I want to know who *you* are."

KATHLEEN: "I am the Feeling that became Fact, the Fact that became Fiction, the Science that became Art, the Germ that became Phenomene. The cycle of rebirth is seeded in my womb. I have borne Athena, Goddess of Wisdom; I have borne the Great Cat Ra. I am a figment of your imagination. I am you, if you will become me."

The movie, script and book build layer after layer, dimension after dimension of what birth of experience can or might be, its success and failure.

Bion (1977) writes of the importance of "wild thoughts" interrupting habitual flow and vicissitudes of linking up with and birthing them. Late in the movie, Man (who sometimes appeared as the Devil or St. Peter) runs proclaiming, "What we need is a criminal act." For William Blake, Satan represented instinctual vitality and Jesus creative imagination, a symbiosis sorely needed to heal egregious splits, although, in some ways, this division itself begins to sound archaic. Late in the script, the Devil and Saint Peter both began to feel they were no longer necessary, as if functions they carried as projections stood some chance of being perceived as psychic tendencies through psychoanalysis.

We have omitted the concern of Priest, P.A. and Scientist with the constitution of the mind, the role of figments, fictions, facts, a concern Kathleen returns to in her self-revelation. It is a theme mentioned on the script's first page that laces the entire *Memoir*, movie, script, and book. One of the most profound concerns in Bion's writing is the fate of emotional reality. It runs through facts, figments of imagination (that Scientist says rule our lives, so much so we may not hear, feel, let in body when it knocks; above, p. 119), phenomena, hallucination, germ, and product (see what I call Bion's O-grams, 1994, pp. 323, 325; Eigen,

2012). Bion adds "somites", which one can take as a unit of experience in the body of the growing foetus, which remains a model for growth of embryonic elements in personality all lifelong. A somatic unit already with feeling content or impact, pressure in the womb of psyche—will it be let in, experienced, born, developed? To what extent? How? The fate of the psyche—is it at stake every moment?

Here is a moment between somites in the womb and Bion's pregnant mother, Rhoda Bion. The somites in the movie are in the form of the nineteen-year-old Captain Bion in uniform lying on a bed in a womb-like container by war trenches, a bible on the bed, mud (mudflats, womb, army trenches) dripping from the straw ceiling. It is as if we hear somites speaking through Mother's and Captain Bion's mind.

MOTHER: "Though the body dies the virus shall live for ever. Did God make a mistake when He allowed the human animal to reproduce?"

SOMITES: "Any foetus could tell you that. I wish you'd stop tossing about."

MOTHER: "How can I help it with you thrashing around?"

SOMITES: "I've got a stomach ache."

MOTHER: "You are my stomach ache."

SOMITES: "I can kick my way out of here easily."

MOTHER: "That pressure on my spine—"

SOMITES: "That pressure on my optic pits—"

MOTHER: "Calm down: I've got an idea you may abort if you kick around like this."

SOMITES: "I am an idea of yours."

MOTHER: "Only an idea?"

SOMITES: "I see a great light."

MOTHER: "It is the darkness of the womb."

SOMITES: "I'm getting absorbed."

MOTHER: "My feelings are getting idea-lised."

Both Scientist and Kathleen as well as pregnant mother, somites, and future young man already at the battlefield of World War One, bear witness to deep interweaving of functions, states, and tendencies of human beings. Feeling runs through it. Freud notes possible historical truths buried in Schreber's delusions and so much illusion and delusion in what we call "reality". Bion repeatedly points out that the study of mind-psyche has a long history but is barely beginning, psychoanalysis a recent midwife in an ongoing struggle.

So often we oppose tendencies that can be co-nourishing. How does capacity to work with aspects of our nature that rip us apart develop? What kind of learning and development is needed to sustain and enrich differences between the many tendencies that compose us while supporting and aiding their creative, life-giving links? It is a quandary that extends to familial and group relationships as well, interweaving psyche, soma and the body politic. I wrote in *Feeling Matters* (2006), "As long as feelings are second class citizens, people will be second class citizen."

Bion's consideration that the emotion in sessions he is interested in is as yet unknown, perhaps unknowable does not make things any easier. But it does add a modicum of humility to the way we approach each other and what we think we know about each other—and ourselves.

A powerful emotional reality made up of sets of realities build as fragments follow one another in what may be chance, unplanned ways but in themselves real happenings, incomplete moments, threaded together by a certain felt sense.

P.A. says at one point in the movie: "This place is thick with fictitious characters! There won't be enough cloud drift for them." Each of these characters carry whole domains of human experience, blends of fact and fiction in the truth of life, perhaps a new kind of freedom growing.

One more interruption, a quote from Grace, a character in a kind of play involving two characters having more or less parallel monologues, Grace and Dr. Z (Eigen 2009, chapter seven). Grace had been hospitalised multiple times and through life and therapeutic work reached a point at which she was hospital and medication free, living at the edge of her creative experience. The Z in Dr. Z comes from Winnicott (1971) writing on infant separation from mother. If mother is away for x time, baby is OK; if away x + y time, baby recovers and comes back together well enough; if x + y + z time, permanent alteration takes place, lasting psychic damage, alteration mentioned by Freud (1937c). The domain of experience investigated by Dr. Z, Grace and Bion is what I all the z dimension.

Here Grace struggles with a sense of something "Wrong", a sense that has been with the human race a very long time (above, pp. 100–101), a sense to which psychosis can be especially sensitive.

GRACE: "I am thinking of the Wrong. It is my essence. I think of a story in the news. A girl killed by her stepfather. She is tied in a chair, eats dog food, beaten, starved. Her mother is in jail weeping, saying she's a good mother. Did the little girl's stepfather and her mother try to kill the Wrong? People try to kill the Wrong but the Wrong kills them. That little girl is in me. I am a lucky her, alive in this room with you, with your Wrong, our wrongs together. We are lucky because we leave each other after forty-five minutes, we dose each other out. Time protects us, lets us tolerate being wrong together.

"Wrong meets wrong. We survive this meeting. In so much real life, meetings blow up, crash, even lead to death. Wrong against wrong, an excuse to kill. War sweeps people along. What led to this little girl's murder? What swept them along? A story said she was rambunctious and instead of giving in, like I did with my parents, she got worse, obnoxious, troublesome—and he killed her. She died rather than give in. I gave in and became crazy and am with you here today.

"Devil inflamed devil. A little girl's energy inflamed tyranny. We are attacked and attack back. A little girl's energy and a maimed adult without resources to meet the Wrong.

"Do we really survive each other here in this office? Not just survive—change? Something happens for the worse. If we go far enough into the worse, we change. Wrong never goes away but something happens when we grip it. I go into your wrong, you into mine. I find mine through yours, you through mine. To touch the worst. Most people most of the time try to get out of it when the job is to get into it. Freedom is working with the Wrong. I feel free when I don't have to make believe I'm right."

Something obscure, unseen, shines. Bion (1991) writes that "the galactic centre of the origin of the universe remains unobserved." He is speaking metaphorically about the emotional centre of the psychic universe. But as Freud writes about figures of speech like a look stabbing my heart or words striking a blow to the face, more than metaphor is involved. Something real is happening, life and death of feeling is at stake, psychic existence is at stake. Metaphor and emotional reality become indistinguishable.

CHAPTER NINE

Changing forms: session excerpts

T om sat for a long time wondering who he is.

I saw myself in him. For a period, when I was younger, I followed a practice in which one stares at a mirror illuminated by a candle in the darkness saying, "Who am I? Who am I?" while watching one's image change forms.

Tom wondered within, feeling himself change identities, uncertain where he would land, if landing was possible.

"Anxiety about death prevents me from living", he said at last. He felt crucified by his life. To take a path and be something or someone felt like dying.

After another silence he said, "It's not the soul being freed from the body but the soul being freed from itself."

The soul is its own torment. I often wonder about doctrines emphasising liberation of spirit from body. The real conundrum is liberating spirit from itself.

There are all kinds of spirits, bad, good, mixed, all kinds of affective attitudes, ways of approaching experience, approaching oneself. Some kill themselves when private hell feels more tormenting than fear of dying.

"I go outside and start to cry", said Tom. "The bright day, life growing in cracks of the sidewalk or on the side of a road. Life wherever it can, however it can."

Your insides to mine, mine to yours, I thought. We create it; it is creates us. "*We* grow wherever we can", I said.

"There is a pain that never stops. It comes and goes. Sometimes you forget about it, it disappears, but just when you remember it isn't there and think it's gone, it comes back. Does it stay in the background or can it be really gone? Gone, as if a switch turns off for a moment, then on. Off-on, gone-here."

A pulsating pain, rhythm of existence. We have a musical body, beating, breathing. I saw a man in a dream leading a line of people in a dance. He seemed awkward, unconcerned what others thought, moving as he felt, forward, side to side. Dancing within, not outside himself. I felt stronger watching him.

I'd like to communicate this feeling to Tom. It's about being one's own person, but first I need to make it my own. It's easy to reduce a moment to what you know instead of letting it take you somewhere you don't.

"I feel a need to be alone this Christmas", Tom said. "It's family time, I know, time to be with loved ones. I'd like to be with others but feel a need to be with myself."

I felt a little scared. During the holidays people feel isolated enough but to stay all by oneself? He spoke of an emotional need, deeper than desire. Bion wrote catastrophe links personality together. Not just a sense of catastrophe but catastrophe itself. I think Tom wants to be alone to feel the catastrophic link.

"There is a hole in my heart", Tom continues. "A lack of love for those close to me. Everyone who comes near vanishes into the hole. I think it is this hole that holds me together."

I think of Freud's dream navel, umbilical to another world. Freud called the psychical world true reality. External reality impinges and makes itself known. Psyche remains a boundless void the outside world carves a place in. Tom wants to befriend the infinite real within, his lost partner in life.

"Aren't you afraid you will vanish in that hole too?" I ask.

"I suspect I partly have. Not here, not there. Gone. I want to be where reality is. I want to be reality."

"Isn't that a name of God?" I wonder. "I will be there." Freud's ego said to the id, "I will be where you are." Ruth said to Naomi, "I will follow you." What counts for Tom is the impossible, the thing itself, the realness of reality. He will be what he will be, psyche becoming.

"Are you telling me I want too much? The tower of Babel?"

I remember a phrase from childhood cartoons: "Reach for the sky." A robber says this when he holds someone up. It is also said about ambition, naïve dreams, and idealism. "The sky's the limit", a code for no limit at all. Another saying, "The higher you go, the greater the fall." Moments of innocence and experience. There may be a high place within no matter how low you go.

"There is another reason I weep", said Tom. "Sensing my life, moved by my own life. The fact of it melds with the sadness of time, awe of existence."

"Do you need to be all alone to feel your life, cry for your life? Don't others add as well as take away?"

"Yes others add. But there is always fear that it will be taken away. Something goes wrong. Good feeling comes and a stone is thrown into it. It gets to a point where fear comes first, a warning, making me careful, guarded. I shut the good off before it can get spoiled. Love scares me.

"When I was little, something bad always happened to good feeling. Not always but often enough to leave a mark of fear. My father would unexpectedly yell. Panic came. So many hurtful things take you by surprise. There are moments when love is stronger and I can enjoy it. But the negative comes and I draw back. You are right—I do disappear in the hole. I pick holes in my skin. Sometimes I pick on other people for no reason, just because I can. Maybe to give them a taste of the pain I feel."

"Maybe to show others the hole? To let others know? So you won't be alone in the hole?"

"I'd be afraid not to be alone in the hole. I pick at my skin because I don't want it to be there."

"It's too much a barrier?"

"No, too visible."

"You want to be invisible?"

"I *am* invisible."

Again I feel a God sense, the beyond within. Not just that he thinks he is God. Not just inflation. But a sense of boundless void that forms our insides. Unknown infinities as building materials.

"I felt critical of a girl I was with. One moment I couldn't believe something so good was happening, the next I kicked it away. When good feeling came between us, I might as well have screamed, "Get away." I can't let my dreams come true because I can't believe a good dream will stay good."

"Do you need it to be always good or can you find ways of riding the waves back and forth, now good, now not so good, bad, now better again?"

"It's not just fear that it will never be good again, that it will be bad forever. I click off. If I'm gone, the worst will be gone. When the worst happens, it will happen without me."

"And when the positive feeling comes, you won't be there either?"

"No, I won't be there—often. But sometimes a surge pushes past me and lifts me with it, a creativity surge. It's not just that something good makes up for the bad. It's something deeper, more a heightened reality. Out of the blue I start writing for hours. It goes on without me. But there are moments I *am* there."

"And then?"

"I am and am not there. Something more than me makes me want to live."

I think of the daemon in ancient Greece, creative power. A primary characteristic of God is creativity. Winnicott's primary creativity, Emerson's creative power, Bergson's creative intuition is built into us. Winnicott imagines that as infants there are moments we feel we are creating the world. We open our eyes, world appears. Did we discover or create it? Is it creating us? Either way, creativity.

Tom swings between pushing life away and affirming inherent creativeness. One moment he is compelled to end something that is building, the next he discovers roots of new beginnings. One moment everlasting darkness, one moment everlasting light. Here, gone.

* * *

TOM: "When I go inside myself I think others see me naked and I feel ashamed. I used to be angrier and say to hell with them, let them think what they like. Now I quiver, as if God almighty is looking through me and there are no covers. Along with shame is fear.

I'm more defenceless than I used to be. I could use anything as a defence against anything. Now I turn to jelly. No, not jelly, that's not it, but some kind of liquidy thing."

M.E.:   "What kind of liquidy thing? Does it have swirls, eddies, unpredictable currents, or is it still, placid?"

TOM: "I was going to say stagnant. But it's more. Stillness is not stagnant. There are unalive things that seem to live, like wires crossing and twining around each other. You wonder how they do that, form designs, attract each other, braid, tie each other. Their tangles seem alive. It's hard to take them apart. You can feel resistance to being pulled away from each other. Are they mating? Like vines on lattice?

"I was moved to terror by a woman at dinner. She showed me photos she took of children in Malaysia, big eyes staring at the camera, happy to be shot, precious instants of recognition. I marvel at her sense of what would take me past terror to another level. Seeing children in a faraway place being noticed made me happy. They blossomed with attention. Her genius made me feel through them. A special blossoming that made me fall in love with my life again. We have a kind of genius inside waiting to be born."

"Perhaps we help each other fan it into life?"

"Yes, I think so. Heightening washes away terror. When I'm in it, I forget the fear. When it breaks down, passes ..."

"Instead of a good aftermath, bleakness sets in."

"After lovemaking, sadness sets in. But it is good sadness, not bleak. But for me, bleak comes too."

"Your love affair with creativity, sad, bleak, fall, uplift."

"Bleakness or fullness. One ends the other. That is my experience. I'm suspicious of it."

"Is it possible for each to hold the other or is it one or the other with no relief?"

"It is the latter, no relief. You make me wonder if both are possible. In reality, both exist. I see that it is not one or the other but it feels that way to me." "Both *are* real."

"I *know* that but will I ever believe it, feel it, live it?"

"You are living it even if you do not yet feel connection between states. For so long, there has been an abyss between states. We will see if something else can be lived."

Religions speak of abyss and plenitude as two ingredients of creativity. Birth after birth.

* * *

TOM: "I want to be a suicide bomber. It must feel so good once the fear is past. To give all without remainder—to give everything. What can be better? You blow up and there is nothing left. You are splatter, gone. I am fascinated with "gone". Zero. No one nowhere. Void. Isn't that a phrase: null and void?

"I think suicide bombing is a special kind of mysticism. You open the unknown. Where are you when you're gone? Where is nowhere? I feel peaceful thinking about it. How can that be? Being ripped apart, blown apart creates peace. Rest in peace they say. Rest in pieces. Whole at last—the great vanishing point. A meditative calm.

"Of course I can pretend to blow myself up. But that would defeat the whole thing. To be here without being here, blow up and survive. That sounds familiar."

M.E.:   "Very close to you. Something you've done over and over. Blown up and survive. How blown up? How survive?"

TOM: "You are right. I blew up as an infant. I blew up at birth. I see myself blowing up instant after instant and coming back partly. Some of the pieces come to life again, some don't. They reassemble themselves oddly to resemble a person. I *do* resemble a person. I am often taken as one. But am I? To what extent, in what ways?"

M.E.:   "I can say the same about myself. Where am I? What am I? Yet one can live very well without knowing the answers, if there are any."

TOM: "I am kissing a girl and as the kiss goes on heaven comes. Touch as a gateway to heaven. I gain entry through loving or pretending to love. Once in I can begin to blow up heaven. I'll have made my way in through love, pleasure, the good God gave me. An infiltrator, traitor. What do you think—worth a try? Imagine, blowing up heaven and be done with it. Does anything tease one more?"

M.E.: "Then you can begin living without feeling there is more or anything better. You can live life as it is."

TOM: "Have you ever noticed how the word lie lies in life? Can you think of other words lie is in? Believe? Relief? Life is filled with lies. That is not new. We know that lying helps us survive. To lie down and not be seen, hidden, and sneak away, surprise. Do you think lying is so important too? What would we be without it?"

M.E.: "Life without lying—what *would* that look like? Do we think God is truth? No lies in God? I think there is something in us that needs to feel purity without lying and since that is not possible we leave it to God. God carries a feeling we have that we cannot realise—and yet we are not truthless. Is it the mixture that tantalises? We blame ourselves for what we give God."

TOM: "Trapped in moments, traps within traps."

M.E.: "I would say, no wonder you want to blow yourself up but I feel you have blown yourself up many times and it has not worked."

TOM: "That is because I blew the wrong me up."

M.E.: "And the right you?"

TOM: "You see, that's the point. There is no right me. No really right me. Just me this way and that way. Right and wrong does not apply—yet the words come, the feelings right-wrong come. They make me unhappy."

M.E.: "I think you are saying they cannot be excised. But can they be modulated?"

TOM: "I'd prefer not adverting to them—but they come. They advertise themselves."

M.E.: "Do we want too much? The impossible?"

TOM: "Wanting the possible is too much."

* * *

TOM: "The urge to blow up heaven is getting stronger. I want to bring hell into heaven. I want to turn heaven into hell."

M.E.: "And hell into heaven? I've read they are indistinguishable."

TOM: "People seem to hate each other across the globe."

M.E.: "And tolerate each other? Love each other?"

TOM: "Not so easy. Maybe there is love deep down. Maybe there deep peace beneath everything. But we are too set in our ways taking care of ourselves. We attack quickly or run. Predator-prey seems part of our genes."

M.E.:   "Pray?"

TOM: "I must confess something I've never told you or anyone. I am afraid to say it. In my heart of hearts I feel very close to God and God close to me, closer than anything in the world. I don't know what to do with that feeling. Sometimes I think it keeps me from being with people. I want to be with God alone. Other people frighten me."

M.E.:   "And fear of God?"

TOM: "That's a rub, yes. You got it. Fear runs through it."

M.E.:   "I feel tears building."

TOM: "Yes, I am crying inside. Crying deeper than all the anger in the world. Maybe crying for all the anger because I feel a deeper love the anger stops. Crying for love. Anger says, "Who are you kidding, Tom! You are bull. Do you really think love is real or is that a wish?" What a frightening voice to have inside, aimed at love, mocking it as make-believe."

M.E.:   "Would you be crying if there were no love in you, no love to cry from?"

TOM: "Yes, you touch it. You hit it. It's the deepest thing in the world, the deepest I know."

We were quiet for a long time. The quiet to me felt like prayer, love felt like prayer—love *is* prayer.

TOM: "Love blew up and nothing was left of it. I thought it vanished totally. Blew up and gone, nothing. Then I began to see little pieces of love left from the explosion, like dust in the air, settling randomly, being blown around by random winds. I think it blew up because it was a torment, a tease, a promise it couldn't fulfil. It blew itself up because it wanted to stop torturing people.

"But I also think it was blown up by a jealous force that cannot settle for anything less than absolute annihilation, cannot tolerate anything outside itself. Only destruction is real or *should* be real. An imperative: The only thing real in life is destruction. Life exists as food for a destructive force.

"I don't know which vision is real. I am lost."

M.E.:   "Perhaps both are real in some way. Perhaps they both dramatise
something that exists, truths that qualify each other."

TOM: "Like look before you leap and he who hesitates is lost? A Mobius
strip, something that cannot be taken apart?"

M.E.:   "Something that can't be taken apart no matter how much you
take it apart."

Tom sobs, the weeping grows. What began as a trickle becomes the well
itself. I feel tearful too. His cries go on for some time. Finally he says,
"I am crying for my life. My life as a whole, like a dying man. They say
when you die your life flashes before you. It's something like that but
not a flash. It's a depth feeling for my life. All the pain, anguish, tears,
hurt. And suddenly I am below the fury, under the hate and I am crying
because—yes—I have to—the crying is coming from the love, irreplace-
able, deeper than anything I know I am."

A wordless court in the soul presides over a shift of balance from
cruelty to compassion. Slight shifts make big differences. Surfaces of the
earth dissolve and I feel processes beyond my ability to describe—more
sensing than seeing although some kind of visibility occurs. "Visible
invisible", "darkness visible", not exactly darkness or formlessness but
vague forms forming, slowly changing.

TOM: "I'm brought to a place I can only wish to sit and feel. A place
I'd rather just stay with, wait on, be with, not ask anything
of, and not ask anything more. It is just what it is, what I am.
A mystery—a freeing mystery. I don't know if I can live from it
or not. But I am grateful it is there. How did we find each other?
Will it really make a difference? Can I destroy it? Is it something?
Is it something I can grow into, grow with?"

CHAPTER TEN

Some biographical notes

I was born in Passaic, New Jersey near the end of the Great Depression. I could see New York City floating in the sky across the Passaic River. When I was a little boy I said to myself, "When I'm big I'm going to go there." As soon as I was able, I played hooky from school to go to the city and see bands and singers. Big bands played in theatres. I saw Charlie Parker, Miles Davis, and Bud Powell at Birdland. After college and a number of false starts, with the help of therapy I finally managed to move to New York City permanently and lived there nearly my entire adult life. By the time childhood ended a highway was built by the river blocking the clean view I had as a child and making it dangerous to cross to the river. Living in Passaic, then an immigrant town, was rich with experience, but I knew I was not going to stay (Eigen & Govrin, 2007).

I came in contact with Buddhism in my last year at the University of Pennsylvania, 1957. A poet, who later became a stock market investor, turned me on to a book by D. T. Suzuki, introduced by Carl Jung, and I loved it, read it and reread it. It became part of me. In *The Psychoanalytic Mystic* (1998) I wrote about the one time I saw D. T. Suzuki and the one time I saw Martin Buber, a few years after college. In the short run, reading Suzuki had a terrible effect on me because I stopped going to classes and sat on the lawn in front of College Hall doing something I imagined was meditation. Luckily, it was too late to stop me from graduating. The administration supported me in face of myself, not the first piece of luck and goodness I experienced at Penn.

Suzuki's was one of a handful of most important books I read in college. Others that had a transformative effect include James Joyce's *Portrait of the Artist as a Young Man* and Plato's *Dialogues*. Joyce exploded and melted language, used words in ways I had not known, shapers of life filled with creative secrets, a new kind of freedom. Plato introduced me to Socrates, who evoked the realness of truth. He was, perhaps, the first person I met who used the word "truth" in a way I could believe. Since early childhood truth seemed a tool of coercion and exploitation. "Tell me the truth and I won't punish you." Even outside my family truth seemed a form of manipulative egocentricity, making me wonder what someone wanted. It was not simply "truth" but the self-centred use of truth that came through. Plato was the only author of books that influenced me in college that I learned about in class (sophomore year). All the rest I found outside the classroom by suggestion or luck. I have an undying respect for universities for enabling this kind of serendipity to happen.

In my junior year of college, I was dumbfounded to find myself invited to join the Philomathean Society and Phi Beta Kappa. My grades in the first two years of school were not sterling. I had to take a remedial math class and my freshman English class was not auspicious, although I learned about Yeats and wrote a paper on his esoteric work, *A Vision*, which intrigued me (the teacher's comments were not enthusiastic, perhaps fearing I was going off the deep end). I was disheartened by psychology and did not do well, although as I came to know myself, I realised I was a natural psychologist but not the kind of psychology taught in school at that time. I was fascinated by demonstrations of frog reflexes, dissections in lab, and reaction time experiments—fascinated but not turned on. There were two paragraphs in the text we used that got me interested. One was on psychoanalysis, the other Gestalt psychology—both touched a chord and I wanted to learn more about each, which in time I did, much more.

"Philomath": a lover of learning. That I was, all kinds of learning. I started going to Philomathean Society meetings by invitation from members and enjoyed their presentations. Students performed *The Great God Brown* (O'Neill) with masks. I sat breathless, mesmerised.

Another time, a Canadian movie of Yeats's Oedipus (also amazing masks). Students and faculty gave talks about what most interested them and this interest was palpable. After some meetings, I was asked to be a member by the teacher who introduced me to Plato (Professor Elizabeth Flower) and spoke about Satan in Milton's *Paradise Lost* for my membership presentation. I can't tell you how natural this felt and how thrilling. The Philomathean Society, founded in 1813, may be the oldest literary society in the U.S. and the oldest student group at Penn. Its motto is, *Sic itur ad astra:* "Thus we proceed to the stars."

Now that I think of it, was it simply Socrates that evoked a sense of truth or did Professor Flower have something to do with it, something in her attitude, feeling, way that provided a context for this evocation to be born, a profound affirmation of the human spirit. It was not the last time a teacher helped me. When I was invited to join Phi Beta Kappa in my junior year, I was at first baffled. True, my grades in my third year improved. It was my best year academically, partly due to my girlfriend transferring from Penn to Michigan (creating a hole I could partly fill with work) and the fact that I could take only courses I wanted, mainly English and philosophy. Gluttony—what pleasure. Clichés about treasures of cultural life—all true. What resources creative mind and spirit give us. "My mind to me a kingdom is" (Sir Edward Dryer). Not just or mainly *my*—but the existence of such capacities as meant by mind-spirit and all who exercise them.

Eventually, I learned it was Professor Morse Peckham who nominated me and strongly supported my membership in face of opposition and uneven grades. I was told he clinched it with the argument, "Eigen is going to write—a lot and well." We were joined in love of creative spirit. But how did he know? At the time, I did not know. If you had told me that someday I would write twenty-four or more books, I would not know who you were talking about. Twenty years later I would have been more than happy to write one or two just to be part of this joyous, agonising love (my first book, *The Psychotic Core*, came out at age fifty). Also at Penn, I became close with Professor Arthur Scouten. We boosted each other's spirits. There are others I could mention (Professor Digby Baltzell) but the list would grow long.

When I was publishing at Wesleyan University, I saw a book by Morse Peckham on its list and wrote to him but he had already passed away, as have all the teachers I mentioned. When I was at Penn my mother wondered why my teachers were so important to me. It was a penetrating question with many facets, preparing me for psychoanalysis. In my junior year one of my roommates began therapy with Henry Elkin in New York City, a fairly recent graduate from the Zurich Jungian Institute. One evening, he told me a dream and Dr Elkin's interpretation and stars opened, bells rang. They have never stopped. I soon read all of Jung and some Freud. At the time Jung was simpatico. It would take time and life for me to appreciate the wonders of Freud and all he gave birth to.

Dreams became a holy grail, with Erich Fromm's *The Forgotten Language* another point of entry. I wrote a paper for Professor Peckham on dream-work in Lewis Carroll's Alice books, particularly *Through the Looking Glass*. Mysterious universes kept beckoning.

When I finished college I began work with Dr Elkin, for me a living Socrates.

We worked together eight years, when his marriage broke up and he left the city to teach at Duquesne. We remained friends when he returned some years later. At first the analysis focused on dreams but Henry began evolving, moving into existential analysis, Melanie Klein and the British school. I learned about Winnicott by "randomly" picking a book to read from Dr Elkin's bookcase, waiting for a session.

In one of those "accidents" of timing, I met Winnicott in London about the same time as Henry left the city, about the same time as I finished a training program in psychoanalytic psychotherapy—all in my early thirties (Eigen & Govrin, 2007). Within a few years, I was teaching the work of Winnicott.

In retrospect, so many things happened in a short time, although then it seemed forever. On the trip I met Winnicott, I visited Julia Neumann in Tel Aviv. Erich Neumann's *The Origins and History of Consciousness* (1954) was one of my bibles. Julia was Neumann's widow, a Jungian who read my palm and told me many things about myself. She felt I was trying to live the second half of life first, substituting the wisdom quest for family and work. It took another decade for her words to bear fruit, aided by sessions with Bion in my early forties. Within four years of meeting Bion, I married and became a father, something I wanted in my twenties but couldn't do. Within five more years, shortly before my father and Henry died, my first book came out, as if becoming a husband and father released the writer.

I seemed to have a knack for meeting some of my heroes shortly before they died. I met Winnicott in 1968 and he died three years later.

My contact with Bion was in 1977 and he died in 1979. When I met them, they seemed active, *alive*, profoundly engaged with psychic realities. Bion seemed stronger physically, a big man, once athletic. They both had an earnest, special intensity. When trying to communicate something, Winnicott left his chair and sat at the end of his therapy couch, hunched over, visibly groping, corkscrew-like, unafraid of awkward intensity, digging into what he was trying to find. A kind of unembarrassed nakedness. I felt relief to see him reaching for a depth he wanted to share. It is, I fear, more novel than one would like to think, to feel unashamed of having a psyche. I felt his very presence affirmed mine. If he could be the kind of person he was, I could be the kind of person I am or might become. A kind of permission: if he could do it, maybe there's room for me too.

My meetings with Bion were more extended, complex, therapy sessions rather than a collegial meeting, although I also attended his talks, lecture and party. I've written about my contact with Bion elsewhere (1999, Eigen & Govrin, 2007), his support, advice, sharing, urging, some of which I mention above. I sometimes use the saying, "A little goes a long way." Indeed—a little can be a lot!

Marion Milner is one love who did not die soon after we met. She lived more than twenty years after our meeting in 1975. We wrote to each other till near the end of her life. I wrote a review of *On Not Being Able to Paint* and the first serious critical appreciation of her work (1977, 1983b). More recently, I reviewed (2014e) her last book, one she still was working on the day she died. I taught the appendix for *On Not Being Able to Paint* for many years, a short psychoanalytic masterpiece. Our contact happened spontaneously. We felt supported by one another, appreciated and understood. She touched me many ways. For example, when I walked down the lane of her house after saying goodbye, as I reached the end and began to walk down the street, something prompted me to turn and look back. And there was Marion, almost forty years older than I, standing on her porch waving to me. Does it sound odd her wave became part of my being, a lasting bit of happiness?

She told me to send the manuscript of *The Electrified Tightrope* (1993) to Clifford Scott, a richly creative man to whom she sent her own work for comment. Scott (1993) reviewed my book, which he liked enormously. I think he was taken with non-verbal aspects of experience, a certain body contact and expressiveness. My intuition told me that for him body and spirit were intimates. After reading my chapters of breathing and the face he exclaimed, "That's where psychoanalysis must go."

I think he was aware of a lack of support in my milieu for the kind of work I was doing and wanted friends to tell me to write more. He ended his review saying, "Some will browse but the perspicacious will read and reread." His support and Milner's thrill in reading my words meant a lot to me. Such people teach me generosity. Much is written now about bad boundaries and destructive aspects of some of the "British school". After non-recognition came idealisation, then devaluation. The psychoanalytic field has its changing fashions and virulent areas. All I can say is my contact with "British school" analysts lifted my life.

Margaret Little sent me a nasty note criticising me for my critique of the term "undifferentiation" in Marion's work. I had doubts Marion really meant undifferentiation but something more like paradoxical monism. When she heard about Little's note, she wrote apologising, saying her friend just could not bear the idea of an attack, but she, Marion knew it was not an attack and wondered if she uncritically took "undifferentiation" from Anton Ehrenzweig (another of her friends) and liked the idea of paradox (which Winnicott uses) and adopted it. She agreed she was trying to express something of a paradoxical I-yet-not-I experience rather than collapse of tension.

However, I later wondered maybe Margaret Little was on to something. Maybe I was a young man trying to clear some space for myself. We kill our elders to make room for ourselves. In my own way, I was trying to touch and express the x that led me to Jung, to Henry and Winnicott and Marion and others.

At that time, some of us were interested in deep, transformative work that had spiritual overtones. Regenerative regression, so to speak, although "regression" may not be the best term. In our vision then, you would try to get back to very early states, primordial being, dip in, regrow. My thinking through of the clinical problem went something like this: if the early state you get back to is undifferentiated, you're in big trouble. Madness and death await. You will remain phobic of your depths. But if the primordial state is paradoxical, I-yet-not-I in Marion's and Saint Paul's terms, the foundations are restorative rather than destructive. My vision was of a paradoxical, co-constitutive sense of self-other spontaneously arising and that this generative feeling gets expressed and symbolised in art and human relations in varying ways. I felt this paradoxical moment to be a core therapeutic experience.

In a sense, I was reaching for and re-finding through my clinical work the kind of deep feelings that led me to the therapy field in the first place. What was happening, without my quite realising it, was a kind of unconscious evolution of the experiencing that marked early moments of awakening, such as those expressed in my encounter with Zen in my senior year of college. I unconsciously was linking the depth feeling I so valued in myself with self-other, I-Thou co-creativeness of clinical work. The sense of primordial co-generativity also provided a way of linking more deeply and fully with other workers.

Some have told me I was brave to seek out and meet the people I did when I was young. I never thought of it that way. It was like my soul was gravitating to points of light in a desperate field, a field which often in New York felt deadening to me. At that time I felt like a drowning man and I was driven to these people—Winnicott, Milner, later Bion—because they expressed something else, an alternative, another way of reaching the psyche. What was happening here—ego psychology, mechanistic structural theory—seemed to suffocate the living psyche.

It was in the late 1950s I saw Suzuki and Buber and met Allen Ginsberg in San Francisco. Suzuki had just been in Mexico with Eric Fromm and was hard of hearing. When someone asked him a question about Fromm he replied, "Who's Eric Fromm?" That caused a ripple. Maybe people thought he was being profound.

As mentioned before, there are cases when a little contact with someone can have a big effect and this was one of them. When someone asked Suzuki about passivity (our milieu definitely emphasised activity) he said, "Passivity, passivity—what's wrong with passivity?" And proceeded to say good things about passive pleasures he gets (Eigen, 1998).

My contact with Eastern and Western "spirituality" was experiential from the outset, *in-spiriting*. Yes, intellectual, imaginative—but it hit me through and through, not just East-West but *my* experience, what got triggered in me, something that happened to me and goes on happening, developing. Once the original face hit me, it's been my companion all my life. I fell in love with original face. For a time, mystical experience was mediated by beat poets. I went off to Mexico where I wrote and played piano, then to San Francisco where Ginsberg read *Howl*. When my kids were old enough, I read Allen's late in life poems to them. Original face came naturally but it took fifty years to hear one hand clapping.

I'm still a beat analyst. I tried to learn whatever I could, getting tastes from all of it. I tried Satchitananda, Trungpa, Muktananda, Maharashi, did Rajneesh's fast breathing. Although I sat with many teachers, my organisational compass was probably Taoism. I really don't try to do anything except stick with what is coming up at the time, if I can. If I'm lucky enough not to be too phony. I just try to make contact with what's there at the moment. I've not tried to integrate anything. I'm not a theorist. For me it's all expressive. Phenomenological. Working out particular moments, psychic tendencies, particular affective attitudes, spiritual movement. I try talking about some of this in *Coming Through the Whirlwind* (1992), which is about overcoming dissociations between spiritual and psychological domains. But that sounds so static when, really, it keeps on evolving, opening dimensions that didn't exist for you before.

My father once told me about a man's face he saw for moments that changed something inside him. The man took care of railroad gates in the country. The sighting was unexpected, unpredictable. They did not meet or speak. It was a look of simple humility, humanity itself, a plain soul touched my father's heart and something shined. I sometimes say, I believe in moments, and it appears there is a background for this.

There is also pain and I suspect the pain of life must have been incorporated in this unknown man's humble look that mediated spirit. My father came from a traumatised and traumatising tradition in Austria-Hungary, from the vicinity of Vienna after the World War One. My mother's father and mother came from Poland. She was born on the lower eastside and spoke Yiddish before English and her mother never learned English. My father refused to learn English in the old country because he didn't want to have an accent identifiable as a "greenie". He learned English when he got here at the age of fourteen—and he didn't have an accent.

Both sides of my family had elements steeped in a sacred tradition. I've written about a rebbe who would come to our home once a year for donations (1993, 2007). There was something about him I loved but didn't understand. I always looked forward to his coming. It wasn't until later I understood that he carried a sense of the holy. He shined with a sense of the holy. Now I have words for the light in and around his face, his glow and halo. My father would drop everything when he came.

My father, though, lived a secular life throughout my childhood, mainly focused on making a living. My mother kept kosher until her mother died, when I was maybe five or six years old. She did it mainly so her mother could visit, but now I wonder, such a deep feeling there. My mother never ate pork. I went to shul on Shabbos and tried to get my father to go but he preferred sleeping late on weekends. Later in his life he davened and chanted the haftorahs (a portion of the prophets sung after the main Torah reading). The fall before he died, he chanted the Yom Kippur haftorah—the story of Jonah—in the immigrant shul downtown in Passaic, where he went as a teen with his father and before we moved to Passaic Park. His father lost a leg on the boat coming over and opened a candy store on River Road in Passaic. He made bathtub gin in the back which he sold to police during prohibition and gave me hard Indian nuts to crack when I visited. My father's mother died in the old country before they could send for her, but his sister came. A difficult life, filled with beauty. Both my parents emphasised simple goodness, doing good. No wonder I was blown away by Plato's idea of the good as basic for everything. My father would say God means good.

The good feeling took many forms. Once it came in a big way when I was two, carried by my father to the hospital at night to get my appendix out. I looked up and saw the stars. I was blown away. I couldn't believe anything like this existed. I didn't know what I was seeing and asked my father who tried to explain they were stars. Was it a downpour of celestial milk? What kind of light was this? Liquid light? The stars outside me were shimmering crystals within me. All trauma and depression fell away and I was lifted to the stars. Such thrilling joy and wonder. Isn't it amazing that something that happens once becomes a reference point for the home base of the self, an undying joy kernel that forever after is a centre of one's being? A centre one's being seeks to re-found itself around.

Another time, a variation, was hearing a clarinet player—this time sound more than vision. A beggar in the Catskills, who came around playing Yiddish music and it made my spine tingle and my heart light up. I said to myself, "I want to do that." I got a clarinet within a year and played and played many years. When my clarinet teacher played a song as my reward after a lesson, I laughed and laughed.

Another moment was kissing Laurel goodnight in high school, soft lips, melding body, warmth, heart. I jumped and danced and shouted and skipped—flew all the way home.

Consciousness of the light as such came later, in my twenties. A lot more pain came too. A moment doubled over in intense emotional pain, entirely into the pain, more and more absorbed by it—then an unexpected opening to light. I wanted it to go on and on. The pain was gone. One moment pain, then light. The light was precious. It was a hard experience, to feel so much pain and go into it and into it then puff, a kind of rupture into light, without warning or expectation. As though intensity of feeling perforated a seal. The pain was real, the light was real. In time I would get to know more about what I was going through, but living it is more important.

There are many gradations of light experiences, spectrums from small inner flames to the great light without location. Some version of light might or might not appear in sessions. There are so many therapy schools and approaches that help people. Much therapy goes on in the dark but once light is experienced it's like a compass or orienting point from which faith arises, a sense of faith hard to undo. It is the simple struggle of faith that is often the nitty-gritty reality of sessions. Faith may be a remnant of light, but keeps on working in the dark, often "blind," with hidden night sensors. The faith of darkness. You learn to work with and within it over time. You can titrate it this or that way but also let it go, like Freud describes—letting the horse lead the rider. There are times you may want to use emotional body English to tilt an experience this or that way. Some people try to re-dream a dream to make it come out better. But something important may be lost by imposing too much. How one relates to an experience can be as important as the experience itself.

The light itself is indestructible. But your approach to it can be destructive. You can become more of a liar, controller, and exploiter. People exploit all kinds of spiritual capacities for economic and ego power. As Jung pointed out, people use spiritual and creative capacities for all kinds of motives.

There are all kinds of openings and closings. Often I am more into the actual contact, the moment when I suddenly feel people more deeply—their facial expression, bodily movement, a feeling or tone of voice. Often they, too, feel a deeper contact. At such moments we interfere less and become mediums of opening.

I suppose there are times one would like to transcend categories and moments when one even seems to do so. But even if one can't escape categories there are many ways to relate to them. Just last week in supervision a young woman was talking about a patient, describing something she was working on. She was saying something about her patient's father that made her patient feel interchangeable with any other daughter. She felt her father would have the same feelings for her or her sisters without discrimination of the special qualities of each. He needed a precious girl baby to feel fatherly towards and any girl baby would ring that bell. We spoke awhile and somewhere along the line, in a kind of aside, I connected her patient's father with Chagall when he lost his wife. He told his son, "Get me another wife, I need another." It almost didn't matter as long as the wifely function is being fulfilled. So she—my good supervisee—says, "Oh, isn't that the paranoid-schizoid position?" Ohhh, and we burst out laughing.

Every analytic fashion does that until the next fashion come along or until people say, "I've had enough of that." It's can be a straitjacket or a new cookbook. A lot of formulations are interesting, rich with reality. But the reality is not the formulation, not simply or only or mainly.

I used to call therapy a kind of psychic gymnasium, a place to exercise one's emotional life and thoughts, imaginings that grow from or around one's feelings. It can be more a matter of stick-to-itness than acceptance. In our society we have hyper-consciousness relating to bodies, bodybuilding, exercising: use it or lose it, no pain, no gain. There is much emphasis on physical muscles but we are in danger of losing emotional muscles. As soon as a kid is brought in to see a psychiatrist, within half an hour he or she may be on medication. There's too little chance to see what people can do, no time to interact with another, to use resources that are internal. There may be a growing loss of capacity to cope, a growing failure to develop and explore psychic resources, a loss of ability to use or even have much of a chance to use one's emotional self. One needs help not just in acceptance of psyche but capacity to stick with it, capacity to use oneself.

Therapy has broadened to the point where you can talk about just about anything and everything—on either side, therapist or patient. If you aren't accepting someone, if there's too little acceptance in the room, that can be talked about. It's amazing how greatly expanded our capacity to talk about what is happening (or not happening) in the room has become. Any affect or attitude and variation can be brought up. But the talk isn't as important as the ability to stay with it. And ability to stay with it varies too. One moment you are with it up to a point, you are able to use your emotional sensor, your feel for something, then you lose it, then it's back and you use it some more, you stick with it and it gets away again, almost a kind of rhythm, back and forth. Being here, not being here, coming back again, breakdown—recovery, losing-finding. Maybe there is understanding and acceptance as part of the background brew but what's more important is somehow letting the patient's rhythm lead, finding that rhythm, even jump-starting it if necessary. Perhaps something of the focus here is the sense that something has gone wrong with the patient's emotional education or emotional rhythm and the ability of the unconscious to support an emotional life. And since that is a human difficulty, it applies to the therapist as well.

It's not a matter of secondary processes retraining or getting better defences or even a shift of cognitive attitudes, important as these may be. What's more important is the quality of unconscious support of life. How does the unconscious support life? How much aliveness and what kind of aliveness can the unconscious support without becoming too destructive, without caving in or blowing its fuses.

The job becomes more like becoming an auxiliary dreamer or dream processor to help jumpstart a person's emotional digestive system, a process in which feelings can be better tolerated, digested, part of a fuller flow, part of deep insides, not just unleashed.

I don't think feelings get digested today. There are massive social pressures to thin feelings out or eject them like missiles at or into others (other groups, individuals, parts of self). Feelings get commercialised, politically marshalled and packaged, turned into money or power, slicked up. Various electronic media and image producing machines speed and spread the resulting packages and programs, so that feelings are used for gain, a kind of widespread psychopathic exploitation of emotional capacity with resulting stunting or warping or numbing or over-excitation of the latter (Eigen, 2006b).

This kind of exploitation and pollution and bullying of emotional resources is fast becoming the rule in economic life, although it's always been a tendency. It often seems that on the individual level and for the body politic there's no emotional digestive system at all right now. Ruptures and eruptions around us express rampant emotional indigestion. Widespread emotional indigestion, psychic bellyaches (let alone heart-aches), moulded by calculation, manipulations, schemes that try to order internal disorder. Malice, fear, and greed wedded to righteous ideological "values". What's needed now more than anything is a worldwide working emotional digestive system. If that could evolve, our feelings for ourselves and each other could evolve too. They go together, our feelings for life, for each other, and unconscious life that can support them.

There are many ways I am many things, a Buddhist, Chassid, Taoist, beatnik, psychoanalyst, mystic, phenomenologist, just plain me, every-day me, struggling me, moments of grace … round and round. One way I will always be a Buddhist is that Buddhism helps mediate the possibility of just being there with your thoughts and feelings with-out holding on to them, letting them come and go, not stopping them. That's deeply important to me and looks like it always will be. But I'm also interested in holding them up, holding them. The first phrase, "holding them up", sounds like a holdup, robbery, or perhaps arresting them (policeman: "Hold up your hands, don't move."), arrested flow. The second—holding—sounds like embrace, staying with, attending, caring. It appears that Buddhist texts do this too, since they have care-ful, minute portrayals of psychological life, taking apart and laying bare skeletons of the psyche.

In a way, Buddhism was a kind of parental figure saying, "You don't have to stop your mind. You don't have to stop anything or indulge it. You don't have to say *"This is it"* and stay there. It was freeing and for-tifying, enabling you to say, "This is what I'm thinking now. It is some-thing awful, violent, terrifying. I could hurt someone or myself. Why not wait a few seconds and see how it looks? See how the self looks in a little while."

If President Bush or Osama bin Laden or Saddam Hussein or Palestinian and Israeli militants could do that, how differently things would look. But they couldn't or wouldn't or didn't do, not in a full way. Not in a way in which the next view or sense or profile cancels or goes beyond the one before. Buddhism gives us this kind of permis-sion, this kind of freedom from inner tyranny. Freedom to alter one's take on what self is or isn't, nullification of one's perch as absolute for oneself or others. What if we could all share this openness together? The ability to wait on oneself is a missing function, just like ability to process emotional life is fast becoming a missing or damaged function (e.g., *Damaged Bonds*, 2001b, on damaged emotional processing).

Any little bit of waiting on or processing experience by analyst, Buddhist, Sufi, whatever walk of life, helps keep alive capacities that normative society is suffocating. Emotional life and our capacity to evolve with it is being depleted by economic power mania with all its pleasure tools, the entertainment and sports industries, technological wizardry. Financial greed has always been with us but our growing technological know-how enables it to reach unprecedented possibilities.

I'm not against power but it should be situated in a larger context rather than act as kingpin of the psyche. There are many kinds of powers. Creativity takes many forms, not just economic. How we talk to each other, touch each other can lift or injure. Aspects of Buddhism and psychotherapy are just two ways we are trying to give something else a chance. Plato called thought an inner dialogue with oneself. The quality of one's relationship to oneself is in jeopardy. Winnicott (1988) writes that psychic democracy is rare. Authoritarian tendencies in emotional life often win the day. How does one lessen the grip of self-tyranny and open to more of the guests in one's psychic home? Democracy of the spirit does not appear to be the dominant voice of the age (Eigen, 2006b).

How do we meet our destructive and self-destructive tendencies seems to be the elephant in the room. In *Rage* (2002), I wrote about our addiction to violence. In *Ecstasy* (2001a), I wrote about an ecstatic core of life, close to my basic personal vision. However, I also examine ecstatic destruction and its importance in our age, when technology and money raise it to new powers. Destructiveness may play a role in human growth but there are ways it blocks our evolution.

Rage is so prevalent in our lives. It is perhaps not an accident it is the first word in the Homeric epics, at the beginning of the western literary canon, an introduction to war, erotic theft, and fury. Nowadays we speak of road rage, which Oedipus shared, murdering the stranger in his path, the stranger at the crossroads (which just happened to be his father). Today there is parochial rage of every sort, individual and group. Ethnic rage, territorial rage, economic rage, image and status rage, work rage. The rape of the United States justice system by the highest court of the land in the presidential election of the year 2000 is a kind of festering judicial trauma and judicial rage is smouldering. Political bullying and psycho-spiritual violence is modelled in the highest places, so that power rages move from top down, not just bottom up (Eigen, 2006b, 2007).

In therapy we get to work with rage in intimate ways. Rage can ruin lives, is ruining lives. Rage ruins relationships, ties with children, damages one's own self. Rage, of course, can be creative, necessary. But in the consulting office we see the private consequences of not knowing what to do with emotional reality, a widespread failure to cultivate resources adequate to psychic life. This is a searing social as well as individual problem. My own calling is to work with individuals, do the best I can in my own life and with those who come my way. I can't help it, that's what I do, my place, my niche. My interest is in working with people directly, working with those who can be helped (by me). But we do have an obligation to diagnose society too and some of us are able to do more than that. We need to support each other's creative efforts on the private or public scene and not waste much time bickering over ideological differences (although nit-picking helps one make a living).

While I feel like a Buddhist, that the focus starts with oneself, I do feel more of a need to speak out, to say something about what is happening as it impacts on me and others, as it impacts on our world, the life we share together. I am still dedicated to the changing moment, the living moment, and the next, and the next. But I also feel more involved with peoples' plights across the world and our own at home. I think it a sin not to speak out at this point, as it would be something like remaining silent in Germany in the 1930s. I don't pretend to have answers or know what is happening. But I feel it would be a sin not to say what I could say and share whatever it is I am able to see, incomplete and distorted as it may be. My faith, my hope is that we are involved in a world group process in which we gradually correct and add to each other. Time will tell if this is wish or reality.

A few days after 9/11 and prior to the Iraq war, I heard Al Gore saying he wasn't sure what we should do next. The next day newspapers put him down for not knowing what to do next. For being cowardly, not taking a stand, waffling. They were saying, "Al Gore never takes a stand!" So his not saying what to do next is seen as cowardly. To me that sounds like a bully press, a bully society.

Maybe all of us should say we don't know what to do next. Those leaders so intent on war should *all* say, "I don't know what to do next!" If we keep on saying that, kept trying to act from not-knowing rather than knowing it all, if we did that, things might be very different.

In my first book, *The Psychotic Core* (1986), and again in *The Electrified* (1993) I wrote chapters on omniscience, how much more devastating acting from a position of omniscience is than mere delusions of omnipotence, since miscalculation linked with unconscious omniscience—thinking one knows more than one actually does—can wreak multi-generational devastation. Omnipotence in the service of omniscience. And *vice versa*. Both delusional. Delusions with all too real consequences.

Such hubris. Such destructive omniscience! But it's not just us. The stance is everywhere. Buddhists kill Buddhists. Muslims kill Muslims. Buddhists and Hindus and Muslims kill each other. Palestinians and Israelis kill each other. One could easily add to the list. There's no innocence in this. It is human co-responsibility.

Maybe you have a picture of us, all of us humans, as being more evolved than we really are. Maybe what's now at stake is our evolving to the point where we can cushion pain with compassion. But that capacity has to evolve individually and collectively.

I was saying that we don't yet have psyches—psychic capacity—that can support the intensity of the thoughts and feelings we have. We do not know what to do with our mental or emotional productions. We don't know how to bring them together. So many feelings, so many thoughts, but how to process them is another matter. Our psychic means of production outstrips our capacity to assimilate what we produce. Psychic and mental digestion must always be incomplete, but maybe we can do a little better.

And since our psyches are not well developed, not really up to what feelings and thoughts demand of them, we get overwhelmed. We give up on the task of growing psychic capacity that can do a better job and turn our attention to other things, like raping the environment, making war, bullying ourselves and each other. Pleasures that turn to violence, that turn out to have a violent core, spurred by psycho-social-spiritual aches or discontents we don't know how to address. Evolution is uneven. A thought without a thinker, for example, or an emotion without a person to process it—it may take another millennium (if we are lucky) for a thinker or feeler (thinker-feeler) to begin catching up with a thought or feeling (thought-feeling).

Neurology is very popular now. Neuropsychology/biology is used as an explanation for thought, disease, chemical imbalances, support of widespread use of medication. I am not against a proper use of medication but am against its burgeoning promiscuity, which I fear depletes and retards developing a much needed capacity to digest feelings and use oneself and others in nourishing ways. One might diagnose the human condition as a disease, but it would not be clear that medication could cure it or that we, human beings, would know how to use the medication we produce. One never recovers from being human.

Even at a neurological or pseudo-neurological level, I don't think we are static. It's almost as if our nervous system teases itself to keep up with the experiences it produces. As if our nervous system has pseudo-pods outside itself, like our consciousness, and it keeps trying to catch up. Our consciousness makes a leap, and then physiology has to rush to support it. It's similar to the situation in which we feel something but our psyche has to grow to support the feeling.

Look at pain as a kind of negative example. If the psyche is too weak or undeveloped to work with that pain, and if it is unwilling or unable to wait on its own development, it may just try to make the pain go away one way or another. It may even try to make itself go away in order to rid itself of experiences it can't support. But sometimes pain has meaning. It sometimes tells one something is off, that one's way of life is hurting. Often violence is an attempt to make the pain of one's life go away. Freud's id, sex and aggression, two ways to make the pain go away, universal escape mechanisms. But the pain doesn't go away or stay away. It gets worse and the means to make it go away get stronger.

In our old brain and autonomic nervous system we are programmed to blot our pain with rage. At least, that is one of our programs, to react to pain or loss of control with anger. Freud got pooh-poohed too quickly on this, when he wrote about the infant reacting to impingement with anger. In one of his formulations, he suggested that the infant first reacts to the external world with hatred. It is as if the infant has an emotional baseline, basic core states from which it reacts against disturbance. Disturbances may come from inside or outside its body, from inside or outside its mind.

An extreme but useful variation on this theme is to picture the infant in a blissful state, a blissful time hallucinated as a perfect moment, timeless bliss. Hallucinated perhaps, but real as long as it lasts. Perhaps a hallucinatory real experience we have from the first days of being alive, in or out of the womb. It is dreadful and dreadfully infuriating when pain breaks this wellbeing up and intrudes on bliss that feels like it should go on forever (a wellbeing that carries its own imperative). Rage and outrage rail against the pain, try to make it go away, blot it out, destroy it. The force of trying to end the pain can cause a lot of psychic damage. To end the pain in a final way, one has to end the psyche, and to end the psyche one has to end one's life. If one remains alive, pain returns and the cycle of anger and rage picks up where it left off. Rage does not solve the problem of pain. Not any more than murder solves tribal enmity. But we do keep trying to murder pain away. We hallucinate murder as a pathway to elation or, at least to free oneself of problems. Cruel elation, cruel pain.

A kind of unconscious magic, as Sartre (1936) describes. Emotions as magical wishes rather than sources of growth and nourishment (although there are ways magical wishes can nourish too): "This will make pain go away. My anger will make it disappear." A baby screams the pain away—for a time. I stub my toe. It hurts. And then I slam my hand down on the table—wham! Nothing like slamming the table that hurt my toe to make the pain go away.

Unconscious wishing as part of a hallucinatory dynamism obliterates reality. It tries to disappear difficulties. Like Tony Soprano says about a problem, "We disappeared him." Someone recounted a dream in which she disappeared a sibling. As she looked at her sibling, the latter started to disintegrate, to disappear. Dream interpretation can take an image like this different ways, depending on what affective attitude is dominant. Looks can kill. And looks can bring someone to life. The woman was caught in the fear that anyone she gets close to would vanish. At the same time, she's furious others aren't there to support her in the first place. A vicious circle. That's where therapy comes in. That's where we start to work.

And what about the hopes of the human race? I am an inveterate hoper. I do think great things are coming—or can come, if. Never utopia but a better world, a better life. An ancient pipe dream? Life is a drama, a tragic drama with comic aspects. The atom bomb is the least of it! We've already shown ourselves we can destroy life. We have all kinds of ways to do that. Destructive alternatives are everywhere. We're terrific at murder, but we're not so terrific at peaceful alternatives, helping, easing the pain of living. We are addicted to trauma in spite of growing awareness of PTSD. There are many for whom helping does not provide enough punch. We have to find ways to make peace fiercely attractive enough, to find peaceful ways that satisfactorily support intensity and enable intensity to be nourishing. The old saw about hell being fun and heaven boring tells us more than we want to or can know. Both are polarities, absolutes, and don't offer much help when it comes to real living, except to include them as part of the mix. How to learn to live with the mix we are is closer to the challenge.

There are increasing numbers of people who want to help, who know their own pain and want to ease suffering. It's a race for the masses now. Maybe there are or will be as many helping as destroying, maybe more. Maybe the helpers will reach a critical mass and tip the balance. It's essential to mobilise the caring instinct now. Unfortunately, destructive impulses seem to have control of the media, popular culture. So many movies, TV programs, video games, ersatz violence making violence fascinating and unreal. Or all too real yet hideously attractive. As if curiosity is wedded to destruction rather than generative aspects of living. Perhaps there is a sense in which people feel destroyed in some elusive ways and stare at, reproduce or magnify a sense of inner destruction. A sense of destruction in which inner-outer fuse. As if curiosity has little left to be curious or sated about except death, and even that has become boring. Even at this point we can act on a personal level. Buddhism, the story of Job, and Bion's F in O teaches it is possible to face anything or develop more capacity to do so. In a way, literally impossible as it is, it is necessary to face everything. Bion's notations F in O and T in O point to an open attitude of faith (F) in face of unknown ultimate reality (O) and unknowable transformative processes (T) that go on in O outside awareness (Eigen, 1993, 1998, 2012).

I am now twelve years older than when the interview that forms the basis of this chapter took place, just before the invasion of Iraq. It was published in its original form two years later (Dimidjian, 2004). I wrote *Age of Psychopathy* (2006b) as a reaction to our government's policies and actions. I'm now almost eighty and work with more dying people and those facing the end of their lives. One individual I wrote about earlier, I called "Smith" (1993, 1996). He was dying of heart disease and he came to me so he could die better. He was able to get the help he wanted and had a better death. He felt he had lived a lie. In our work he made contact with what he called *the lie*. Doing that gave him a sense of being at one with himself. More recent accounts of work with dying people, even days from the moment of death, can be found in *The Birth of Experience* (2014b) and *Faith* (2014c). An earlier depiction is in *The Sensitive Self* (2004b), the same year the original version of this chapter was published.

As I've gotten older my practice has gotten older with me. I have a lot of patients a long time, some forty years. Some people need long term contact. There is so much damage that they need a supportive bond that can go on a very long time, sometimes the rest of their lives. I think it cruel to deny people this kind of contact if they need it. A shorter but telling version of this happens with children. The mother who takes her child out of therapy because, "He is getting dependent on you." Well, I've always wondered, what's wrong with that? You want him dependent on drugs, medication, on your absence, on your controlling presence? What is wrong with being dependent on another human being as long as that is needed and useful? I also have patients who come and go more quickly and people of varied ages. I like a garden variety practice. It's a mystery who comes, who stays, and who goes. The unknown is a big part of our work.

* * *

When I was younger, I used to be terrified of death. It dawned on me very early that I would die. I saw my uncles carry my grandmother out of her house when she died. Afterwards, I kept seeing her in different places and told my mother, her daughter, who kept saying that wasn't possible but sometimes almost believed it. I was under five years old. When I was twenty-one, my ten year old brother was killed by a truck. During my teens I had acute terror of dying. I had friends who became suicidal, depressed. I wasn't depressed over my certain death but very scared. Maybe one reason I sometimes see patients so long is to undo my brother's death, forestall death, as well as make life better.

As I entered my twenties, I did not expect that fear to go away. I said, "OK, if that's the way it is, I'll live with it." But it did go away in a kind of miraculous way. It went away in an instant in my early thirties. I was with my Aunt Bert when she was dying, visiting her in the hospital. I was holding her hand and she was telling me how bitter she was, how she didn't expect this to happen, it took her by surprise. I was just sitting, holding her hand, listening. I was looking at her and suddenly I couldn't feel where life left off and death began. It was an experience, not a thought. It just happened. Suddenly, I felt there wasn't much of a difference somehow. A state not against death, not against life, not for either of them. It was a sense that I entered a transitional space of no boundaries. Freud made the remark that he wouldn't be surprised if there wasn't such a great caesura between pre-and post-birth life as we thought. And that's what I felt that day. The terror was gone. Analysis hadn't diminished this terror. This experience wasn't anything analytic.

It was just looking at my dying aunt, hearing her express her fears, her anger, just staying there holding her hand. And all of a sudden, the death terror was gone. I'm not eager to die, but I don't fear it the way I used to. My father felt that death is part of the natural cycle of things and now I felt something like that too. Nearly fifty years after that moment with my aunt, I feel the closer to death I get, the more opens.

I'm thinking of a scene that may not seem apt at first glance. A woman who got raped in southern France. While it was happening she thought, "God, do with me what you will as long as it helps me love you more." That's not exactly my feeling, but there's overlap. God, you put me in this universe. As long as I have such experiences, as long as I love you, as long as my heart keeps opening, it's a mystery why you've done this, all this pain, injury, agony, suffering, yet I feel closer to a presence, a wordless intimacy, and inside myself there is profound embrace.

* * *

My father had a good death, my mother a bad death. My father's death was part of what turned me on to Judaism as an adult or, at least, intensified my relation to it. I always had a Jewish sense which deepened through my father's death. He died twelve years before my mother. I visited him once a week in the hospital in Connecticut where my sister lived. I would bring tapes of music or whatever I thought might be meaningful. One week my mother, sister and I were together in the hospital room, my father in a coma and my sister's rabbi came in. The rabbi thanked my father for the support my father gave him when he was a young rabbi. The rabbi said to my father, "When you were there, I knew there was at least one person who understood me." Then he chanted the sh'ma, the closing prayers at Yom Kippur before the long shofar blast, the Cohanic blessing in the ancient Holy Temple, lines from Adon Olam (the last hymn of the Sabbath morning service—"I place my spirit in His care, when I wake as when I sleep; God is with me, I shall not fear, body and spirit in His keep"), and finally the traditional, "The Lord has given and the Lord has taken away"—in Hebrew, which my father knew long before he learned English. Before the rabbi's last words faded, I became aware my father passed away. He had been waiting for this. When the words came, he could go. He was lovely. He looked perfect. He had a germ of holiness I valued so much.

The rabbi left without knowing my father died while he was singing. While I was standing at the side of the bed, the words came to me in an authoritative, moving way, "The Lord of Abraham, Isaac, and Jacob lives."

The night of my father's funeral I began going to shul and soon began studying with the sons of the rebbe whose holy glow touched me in childhood. They were still alive, old men themselves in Brooklyn, not far from where I lived. My contact with mystical Judaism deepened. I went through an orthodox phase which was beautiful while it lasted. It was really too much for me and my family. My life couldn't support it. My wife's common sense saw us through. Deep contact with a mystical dimension of life continues to ripen, partly fed by Jewish roots, but beyond institutional frameworks.

* * *

How does change happen? How did it happen through the deaths of my Aunt and father I write about above? I'm not sure I can say. And in psychotherapy? What is it that draws us on, leads us on? I've tried depicting what I can in books I have written, now twenty-five of them. What am I trying to say? What am I trying to communicate? Whatever one says, there is something else one could say, something one can't say.

What place can sincerity or devotion have in a psychopathic world? I have a rough time with some of my patients, but overall I am devoted to them. Some are loaded with toxins, self-hate, anger. But whatever tastes I get are nothing compared to what they live. There comes a time when one no longer can blame the intrinsic pain of life on oneself or others. Prayers talk about the miracles of everyday and I have experienced the reality of such miracles in therapeutic work. There is danger to positively and negatively idealise, make something better or worse than it is. How do we measure? We undergo many incarnations, even in a short life, and all spiritual paths have threads that value what is most precious in our core.

Even if we are hard put to say exactly why this happens and not that, why or how this person benefits a lot or a little, we best follow Buddha's advice and keep practicing. Keep on doing it, this mysterious process in which one being touches another and one touches oneself. As we do it something grows richer. *We* grow richer. More keeps happening. Paths, dimensions, experience open. There is no answer, only more to do and feel.

No tricks. Just working, finding, feeling, thinking, communicating, keeping at it. Sometimes it feels like we're monkeying around in the basement or sometimes working with the flow the psyche is. Psychic respiration, circulation, digestion. How a person affects another or affects oneself. Quality of attunement is only a start. It's a treacherous business. So much can go wrong anytime and if we are lucky, we work with what goes wrong. I think of Asian carpets weaving errors into art.

I was once talking to a very sensitive man about the snaking directions of the Passaic River, this way, that, almost turning its flow back to where it started. As I was growing up, it became so polluted you wouldn't want to swim in it. In response, he began speaking to me about how left to itself, the river would cleanse itself over a long enough time. And I thought of the Taoist *wu-wei*. It had not occurred to me the river could be self-cleansing. Life is so often associated with dirty processes, but generative faith runs deeper. It's part of the paradox of living to keep the long view in mind while giving all you have to what you can do now.

Water finds its way around barriers. There is more to life than any life can exhaust. It is not necessary to make believe that things are better than they are in order to give yourself fully to the plenty in front of you. It's not fair that evil keeps us busy, but it does. Yes and no is part of every experience but I'm a hopeless romanticist feeling yes more deeply. The major problem that faces us as a human group as well as individuals is harm we do to ourselves and each other. No spiritual, political, economic, psychological path has a solution. No matter what we claim, so far there is no good reason to trust ourselves to know what help might be. A world acceptance of such an attitude or realisation might itself be a salutary beginning.

Book review: *On Not Being Able to Paint*. Marion Milner. New York: International Universities Press, 1973

Marion Milner, a friend and colleague of D. W. Winnicott's who profoundly influenced him, offers an extremely rich account of her journey as a "Sunday painter". In this work, first published over twenty years ago, she depicts in personal terms how she gradually let go of stereotyped ideas of reality, painting, and the corresponding experiential rigidities in order to tap deep processes of psychic creativity. She is a psychoanalyst and painter who uses her art and analytic work in ways that stimulate and amplify each other and contribute to the basic art of self-building.

Her encounter with her own creativity amounts to a dialogue between the creative process and psychoanalysis, in which the latter throws light on the former but is itself transformed by the demands the phenomenon of creativity makes on a theory. Psychoanalysis helps Milner understand her fears related to her experience of painting. It helps her create a link between herself and her products, bolsters her courage to keep moving further, and provides an orienting compass as new areas unfold. At the same time the creative process and products encountered by psychoanalysis extended, deep, and possibly turn it inside out. It becomes clear in the course of this honest spiritual autobiography that the phenomenon of creativity has radical implication for psychoanalytic theory.

Some resistance to the creative process can be caused by superego-generated inhibitions. Internalised parental prohibitions and threats hamper and skew productions. At this level productions of monsters and other cruel forms objectify incoming aggression which tends to become self-directed. Self-attack reflects attacks once made on one by others, and drawings of bad figures ultimately are representations of bad or demonic others.

On the other hand, the infant also has knowledge of its own aggressive, rapacious wishes. He has insatiable desires which provoke his rage even with the best parenting. According to Milner, here following Melanie Klein, the baby's knowledge of his own destructive impulses is a more implicit source of guilt, a part of the human condition. In this context the infant projects his own hate onto the superego as well as turning it more immediately back upon himself out of fear and guilt. Here monsters and other cruel forms represent id impulses and self-blame. In true Kleinian style, art can act as reparation, a way of repairing self and others. It is a love gift to make up for destructive desires, to make amends (to mend).

At this point, however, Milner attempts to go deeper than Klein and points to a preambivalent source of creativity. The deeper meaning of the self-defeating dramas initiated by oral incorporation is the intention to forestall or undo the development of otherness. By attempting to incorporate the other, one retains a sense of fusion or oneness. For Milner a feeling memory of a phase of predifferentiated oneness underlies the feeling of wholeness in life. It is this sense of wholeness that art most basically attempts to recreate. One may resist creative impulses in order to ward off the feared ego loss that regression to a more undifferentiated state would entail. In this context psychic flexibility involves working through the double anxiety of separation and union.

If the sense of wholeness is an illusion, it is a necessary one. Milner points out that the very foundation and evolution of selfhood depends on it. For the world to take on viable meaning the ego must maintain contact with its imaginative core and find ways of linking its psychic creations with material reality. Milner also develops the notion of the "imaginative body", a bodily felt way of living oneself into situations or objects and elaborating and transforming them. The imaginative body avoids usual forms of conceptualised thought and physical action. It is adventurous, receptive, and spatially oriented, and in effect it involves an active exercising of the essentially mystical experience of subject-object union, the nuclear sense of wholeness. In sketching some of the functions of illusion and some of the working of the imaginative body, Milner offers stimulating hints for a view of perception as a form of imagination. The splitting off of perception from imagination may result in psychic depletion or more gross forms of pathology. Psychic health requires the uplifting, dialectical play of illusion and imagination with the hard facts of life.

The above ideas lead to a revision of the psychoanalytic theory of symbolism. Symbols of unconscious concerns point not only or even most essentially to id representations but to the ego's own self-experience, mainly its sense of underlying wholeness. At the heart of this experience is the ego's experience of creativity itself. In some sense art recreates this peak experience of life. It is fundamentally ecstatic-orgasmic in a way that broadens our idea of orgasm and makes genital orgasm into one of a variety of possible orgasmic experiences that connect with the ecstatic sense of ideal unity. These ideas imply that a theoretical account of human development must take the sense of wholeness as its centre or starting point. Revisions of psychoanalytic theory by such authors as Balint, Fairbairn, and Winnicott are among those that attempt to do this.

Unfortunately the functional concept Milner uses to articulate "wholeness"—undifferentiated union—remains vague and undoes itself. There is a general problem in using the idea of undifferentiated states, since to be undifferentiated and still exist seems impossible. Gestalt psychology, for instance, has shown that some differentiation must be present for perception to occur. To exist at all differentiation is required. The task becomes one of describing the kind or kinds of differentiation which give rise to the experience of unity, a differentiated unity. This requires a more detailed and comprehensive explication of the relevant primordial self-other relationships. A more comprehensive developmental framework would also be needed to adequately encompass the distinctions Milner makes between physical experience, the imaginative body (felt imaginative perception), everyday perception, more purely observing functions, and ratiocination. At the least Milner's work indicates that far more thinking about imagination and its varied relationships with perception is sorely needed and that the implications of such an undertaking are far-reaching.

In addition to refocusing analytic theory, Milner deepens familiar analytic findings. She underlines the critical importance of the psychodynamics of anality in creative work and makes important contributions in this area. She also enriches the meaning of the primal scene as symbolic of creative action. Throughout the book she concerns herself with problems of mind-body integration and interactions between thinking and feeling. For her, creative impulses grow out of body feelings, and consciousness suffuses the body. In her descriptions she adds not only to theory but also to our capacity to experience on many levels. The fact that she cannot and does not try to solve the problems her formulations imply does not lessen the value of her descriptions. On the contrary, one gains a sense that when one works with the core problems of human existence, fruitful things happen and, similarly, when one follows the thread of experience deeply enough, the basic problems spontaneously emerge.

Michael Eigen (1977). *The Psychoanalytic Review*, *64*: 312–314.

Book review: *Bothered by Alligators*. Marion Milner. London: Routledge, 2012

Bothered by Alligators is a lovely book that is more than lovely. It is filled with practical wisdom for living, warts and all. This is Marion Milner's last book, one she worked on in her nineties and was still getting ideas for sitting in bed the day she died at the age of ninety-eight.

It started when she found picture-stories her son, John, made when a child and a diary she kept at that time. One thing she wondered about was how John's storybook was touched by her maternal depression. In the first four parts of the book we are treated to back-and-forth explorations of John's storybook linked with Marion's diaries.

I hope you forgive me for using her first name here. I feel uncomfortable being formal. Marion and I met in 1975 and corresponded until near her death. She shared with me personal difficulties as well as creative concerns. We were, I feel, very supportive to one another. In 1977 I reviewed *On Not Being Able to Paint* for this journal. It touched the co-generative arising of a sense of self and other, which plays a role in our sense of generativity. In 1983 I published the first serious, extended exploration of her work.

She sent her early manuscript to me and Clifford Scott, asking for our thoughts about publication. She was hesitant for several reasons, one being how much she reveals about emotional states of mother and child, as well as laying bare marital problems of the time. Scott and I were both supportive and encouraging, to say the least. John gave full permission.

I just learned from the published book that she entered analysis with Scott after leaving Winnicott. Scott told her she never had an analysis. Her analysis with Scott ended after two years, when he returned to Canada. As an aside, she told him to review my work, *The Electrified Tightrope* (Eigen, 1993), when it came out, which he did for the first volume of the *Canadian Journal of Psychoanalysis*.

Another aside I learned from reading this work is that Adam Phillips's (1989) book *Winnicott* helped her see some of Winnicott's difficulties that may have affected their analysis. Phillips edited *The Electrified Tightrope*, and perhaps that added a little more push to Milner's suggestion to Scott.

I had always thought she was a mentor to Scott and did not realise he was her analyst for a time, a special time, for leaving Winnicott was an intense struggle. She wept throughout their last session. When he conveyed to her how special she was to him, she felt, "I don't want to be special, I want an analysis."

Many of you touched by Winnicott will find special enjoyment in a part of the book called "D. W. Winnicott and me," which includes three chapters: "Being in analysis with D. W. Winnicott", "A Winnicott paper on disillusion about what one gives", and "D. W. W.'s doodle drawings". Apparently a good deal of fluidity existed between certain analysts and patients, with positive and negative dimensions (Eigen, 1981b).

The book covers a lot of territory yet does not feel rushed. It is all expressive of Marion's life experience, the feel of life, its riches and problems. She tells the story of her early upbringing, her father's breakdown when she was young. She writes about her interest in creativity, painting, and deepening aspects of unconscious processes. Each step of the way she shares observations, insights, experiences that add to our feel of creativeness and appreciation of details of our own lives. For, if one follows Marion, one reaches an unavoidable sense of the richness of being a psychical being.

She has a special sensibility, an affinity for reaching a depth point where the difference between psychology and spirituality fades. She tells us of many psychospiritual exercises she did, many of them arising spontaneously, others culled from readings and learning experiences with others. Many of the meditative exercises she did were simple yet multidimensional, spanning word, image, and body feeling. Often they left her with a fresh sense of life, new sensitivity to the present moment. I especially liked the way some of them arose in response to special difficulties she was having in particular situations, as, for example, when she felt her anger or sadness was getting in the way of something fuller. In parts of Milner's work, one feels the distance between spirituality and psychoanalysis melt, as both link to open life.

The last part of the book is called "Towards wholeness" and includes a chapter, "Towards bringing bits of oneself together". In another chapter she writes of the need for fiction. She warns against a literalising tendency that can diminish the range of experiencing. The last chapter of this section is "An area for the play of opposites." But the book does not end there. She adds a "Conclusion" on "useable dreams", and you feel the book could go on and on. And you are one of the vehicles for it to go on and on in your own feel for life. Is it paradoxical that the work of an individual so into her own experience leaves us with a sense of shared psyche, a renewed appreciation for our own processes as well?

It appears Marion saved much of what she did, perhaps archived her work in some way, at least had it somewhere around for her to go back to. This, too, adds to appreciation of our lives, she so values hers. She returns to a happening, an image, a phrase, over and over, and it grows in meaning and texture. In her nineties she cut up old paintings and made collages out of the pieces. One gets a feel, by example, how many ways bits of our lives can become part of shifting, growing tapestries of the whole.

I felt the editing of this book was wonderful. It includes colour plates of John's entire picture-storybook, some of Marion's paintings, and a photo of John as a child. Years ago I asked Adam Phillips how Marion's manuscript was coming. He told me he doubted it ever would be together enough for publication. Now, fourteen years after her death, the book we are given sings. The fragmentary nature of some of its parts adds a breath of fresh air, a certain area of freedom. I have always been attracted to fragmentary writing. But this book adds up to more. Marion's unassuming tone moves throughout the work, adding to a sense of life working with its parts. The whole may be greater than the sum of its parts, but the parts give the whole everything.

Michael Eigen (2014). *The Psychoanalytic Review*, 101: 129–131.

REFERENCES

Balint, M. (1968). *The Basic Fault*. London: Tavistock.

Bateson, G. (1972). *Steps to an Ecology of Mind: Collected Essays in Anthropology, Psychiatry, Evolution, and Epistemology*. Chicago, Illinois: University of Chicago Press, 2000.

Beier, M. (2006). *A Violent God-Image: An Introduction to the Work of Eugen Drewermann*. New York: Bloomsbury Academic.

Ben-Shahar, A. R., Oster, N, & Lipkies, L. (forthcoming, 2016). *Speaking of Bodies*. London: Karnac Books.

Bergson, H. (1998). *Creative Evolution*. Mineola, NY: Dover Books.

Bion, W. R. (1965). *Transformations*. London: Karnac, 1984.

Bion, W. R. (1970). *Attention and Interpretation*. London: Karnac, 1984.

Bion, W. R. (1977). *Two Papers: The Grid and Caesura*. London: Karnac, 1989.

Bion, W. R. (1991). *A Memoir of the Future*. London: Karnac.

Bion, W. R. (1994). *Cogitations*. F. Bion, (Ed.). London: Karnac.

Bohm, D. (1980). *Wholeness and the Implicate Order*. London: Routledge.

Buber, M. (1958). *Moses: The Revelation and the Covenant*. New York: Harpers Torchbook.

Chuang Tzu (1964). *Chuang Tzu: Basic Writings*, B. Watson (Trans.). New York: Columbia University Press.

Coltart, N. (1993). *Slouching Towards Bethlehem*. London: Free Association Books.

Coltart, N. (1995). Review of *The Electrified Tightrope*. *Winnicott bookshelf Spring No. 10*. London: Winnicott Studies.

Coltart, N. (1996). *The Baby and the Bathwater*. London: Karnac.

Dimidjian, V. (2004). *Journeying East: Conversations of Aging and Dying*. Berkeley, CA: Parallax Press.

Ehrenzweig, A. (1971). *The Hidden Order of Art*. Berkeley: University of California Press.

Eigen, M. (1974). Fear of death: A symptom with changing meanings. *Journal of Humanistic Psychology, 14*: 29–33.

Eigen, M. (1977). Book Review: *On Not Being Able to Paint* by Marion Milner. *Psychoanal. Rev., 66*: 3–8.

Eigen, M. (1981a). Comments on snake symbolism and mind-body relations. *American Journal of Psychoanalysis, 41*: 70–73.

Eigen, M. (1981b). Guntrip's analysis with Winnicott—A critique of Glatzer and Evans. *Contemp. Psychoanal., 17*: 103–111.

Eigen, M. (1983a). On time and dreams. *Psychoanal. Rev., 70*: 211–220.

Eigen, M. (1983b). Dual union or undifferentiation? A critique of Marion Milner's view of the sense of psychic creativeness. *Int. Rev. Psycho-Anal., 10*: 415–418.

Eigen, M. (1986). *The Psychotic Core*. London: Karnac, 2004.

Eigen, M. (1992). *Coming Through the Whirlwind*. Wilmette, Il: Chiron Publications.

Eigen, M. (1993). *The Electrified Tightrope*. A. Phillips (Ed.). London: Karnac, 2004.

Eigen, M. (1995). *Reshaping the Self*. London: Karnac, 2013.

Eigen, M. (1996). *Psychic Deadness*. London: Karnac, 2004.

Eigen, M. (1998). *The Psychoanalytic Mystic*. London: Free Association Books.

Eigen, M. (1999). *Toxic Nourishment*. London: Karnac.

Eigen, M. (2001a). *Ecstasy*. Middletown, CT: Wesleyan University Press.

Eigen, M. (2001b). *Damaged Bonds*. London: Karnac.

Eigen, M. (2002). *Rage*. Middletown, CT: Wesleyan University.

Eigen, M. (2004a). A Little Psyche-Music. *Psychoanal. Dial., 14*: 119–130.

Eigen, M. (2004b). *The Sensitive Self*. Middletown, CT: Wesleyan University Press.

Eigen, M. (2005). *Emotional Storm*. Middletown, CT: Wesleyan University Press.

Eigen, M. (2006a). *Lust*. Middletown, CT: Wesleyan University Press.

Eigen, M. (2006b). *The Age of Psychopathy*. Available online at www.psychoanalysis-and-therapy.com/human_nature/eigen/pref.html

Eigen, M. (2007). *Feeling Matters*. London: Karnac.

Eigen, M. (2009). *Flames from the Unconscious: Trauma, Madness and Faith*. London: Karnac.

Eigen, M. (2010). *Eigen in Seoul, vol. 1: Madness and Murder.* London: Karnac.
Eigen, M. (2011a). *Eigen in Seoul, vol. 2: Faith and Transformation.* London: Karnac.
Eigen, M. (2011b). *Contact with the Depths.* London: Karnac.
Eigen, M. (2012). *Kabbalah and Psychoanalysis.* London: Karnac.
Eigen, M. (2014a). *A Felt Sense: More Explorations in Psychoanalysis and Kabbalah.* London: Karnac.
Eigen, M. (2014b). *The Birth of Experience.* London: Karnac.
Eigen, M. (2014c). *Faith.* London: Karnac.
Eigen, M. (2014d). Non c'è nessun no. ["There is no no"]. *Psiche: Rivista di cultura psicoanalitica, 2*: 307–319.
Eigen, M. (2014e). Book review: *Bothered By Alligators* by Marion Milner. *Psychoanal Rev. 101*: 129–131.
Eigen, M. (2015). My session with André. *Psychoanal. Rev., 102.*
Eigen, M. & Govrin, A. (2007). *Conversations with Michael Eigen.* London: Karnac.
Elkin, H. (1958). On the origin of the self. *Psychoanal Rev., 45*: 57–76.
Elkin, H. (1972). On selfhood and the development of ego structures in infancy. *Psychoanalytic Review, 59*: 389–416.
Fairbairn, W. R. D. (1954). *An Object-Relations Theory of Personality.* London: Routledge, 1994.
Federn, P. (1926). Some variations in ego feeling. *International Journal of Psycho-Analysis, 7*: 25–37.
Freud, S. (1900a). The interpretation of dreams. *S.E.* IV & V. London: Hogarth.
Freud, S. (1911c). Psycho-analytic notes on an autobiographical account of a case of paranoia (dementia paranoides). *Standard Edition 12*: 3–82. London: Hogarth.
Freud, S. (1918b). The history of an infantile neurosis. *Standard Edition 17.* London: Hogarth.
Freud, S. (1920g). *Beyond the Pleasure Principle. Standard Edition 18*: 1–64. London: Hogarth.
Freud, S. (1925a). A note upon the "Mystic Writing Pad". *Standard Edition 19*: 226–232. London: Hogarth.
Freud, S. (1937c). Analysis terminable and interminable. *Standard Edition 23*: 216–253. London: Hogarth.
Freud, S. (1963). *Psychoanalysis and Faith: Dialogues with the Reverend Oskar Pfister.* H. Meng & E. L. Freud (Eds.). New York: Basic Books.
Green, A. (1975). The analyst, symbolization and absence in the analytic setting (on changes in analytic practice and analytic experience) *International Journal of Psycho-Analysis, 56*: 1–22.
Green, A. (1996). *On Private Madness.* London: Karnac.

Green, A. (2011). *Illusions and Disillusions of Psychoanalytic Work*. A. Weller (Trans.). London: Karnac, 2008.

Grotstein, J. (2007). *A Beam of Intense Darkness: Wilfred Bion's Legacy to Psychoanalysis*. London: Karnac.

Grotstein, J. S. (2000). *Who is the Dreamer Who Dreams the Dream: A Study of Psychic Presences*. New York & London: Analytic Press.

Klein, M. (1946). Notes on some schizoid mechanisms. In: *Developments in Psycho-Analysis*. M. Klein, P. Heimann, S. Isaacs, & J. Riviere (Eds.). London: Hogarth Press, 1952.

Lacan, J. (1977). *Ecrits*. A. Sheridan (Trans.). New York: Norton.

Lacan, J. (1993). *The Seminar of Jacques Lacan Book III: The Psychoses 1955–1956*. J. -A. Miller (Ed.). R. Grigg (Trans.). New York: W. W. Norton & Co.

Matt, D. C. (1996). *God and the Big Bangy: Discovering Harmony between Science and Spirituality*. Woodstock, VT: Jewish Lights.

Matte-Blanco, I. (1975). *The Unconscious as Infinite Sets*. London: Duckworth.

Matte-Blanco, I. (1988). *Thinking, Feeling and Bring*. London: Routledge.

McCurdy, H. (1961). *The Personal World*. New York: Harcourt Brace Jovanovich.

Meadow, P. W. (2003). *The New Psychoanalysis*. Lanham, MD: Rowman & Littlefield.

Meltzer, D., Brenner, J., Hoxter, S., Weddell, D., & Wittenberg, I. (1975). *Explorations in Autism*. London: Karnac.

Merleau-Ponty, M. (1965). C. Smith (Trans.). *The Phenomenology of Perception*. London: Routledge & Kegan Paul.

Milner, M. (1957). *On Not Being Able to Paint*. London: Routledge, 2010.

Milner, M. (1973). *On Not Being Able to Paint*. New York: International Universities Press.

Milner, M. (1987). *The Suppressed Madness of Sane Men: Forty-four Years of Exploring Psychoanalysis*. London: Routledge.

Milner, M. (2012). *Bothered by Alligators*. London: Routledge.

Molino, A. (1998). *Freely Associated: Encounters in Psychoanalysis with Christopher Bollas, Joyce McDougall, Michael Eigen, Adam Phillips and Nina Coltart*. London: Free Association Books.

Moncayo, R. (2012). *The Signifier Pointing at the Moon: Psychoanalysis and Zen Buddhism*. London: Karnac.

Neumann, E. (1954). *Origins and History of Consciousness*. London: Routledge, 1999.

Philoctetes Society (2007). "What is guilt?". Available to view online: http://www.youtube.com/watch?v=BRCHM6AqM&list=UUsOC2DDJ 888NEr0gSPVl4TQ

Phillips, A. (1989). *Winnicott*. Cambridge, Mass.: Harvard University Press.

Read, H. (1955). *Icon and Idea*. Cambridge: Harvard University Press.

Reiner, A. & Panajian, A. (Forthcoming, 2016) *Of Things Invisible to Mortal Sight: Celebrating the Work of James S. Grotstein*. London: Karnac.

Sartre, J. -P. (1936). *The Imagination*. K. Williford & D. Rudrauf (Trans.). London: Routledge, 2012.

Schneerson, M. M. (1978). *On the Essence of Chassidus*. Y. Greenberg & S. S. Handelman (Trans.). Brooklyn, NY: Kehot Publication Society.

Schneerson, M. (1998). *On The Essence of Chassidus*. Y. Greenberg & S. S. Handelman (Trans.). Brooklyn, NY: Kehot Publications Society.

Scott, W. C. M. (1993). Book review: *The Electrified Tightrope* by Michael Eigen. A. Phillips (Ed). *Canadian Journal of Psychoanalysis 1*: 149–153.

Shahani, K. (1983). *A Memoir of the Future* (movie fragments). Available online: www.youtube.com/watch?v=MKVS7hhqUL4&feature=you tu.be).

Soler, C. (2014). *Lacan—The Unconscious Reinvented*. London: Karnac.

Spotnitz, H. M. (2004). *Modern Psychoanalysis of the Schizophrenic Patient: Theory and Technique*. New York: YBK Publishers.

Tomlin, E. W. F. (1952). *The Great Philosophers: The Eastern World*. London: Skeffington & Son.

Werner, H. (1940). *Comparative Psychology of Mental Development*. New York: Harper & Brothers.

Winnicott, D. W. (1953). Transitional objects and transitional phenomena. *International Journal of Psycho-Analysis, 34*: 89–97.

Winnicott, D. W. (1971). *Playing and Reality*. New York: Basic Books.

Winnicott, D. W. (1974). Fear of breakdown. *International Review of Psycho-Analysis, 1*: 103–107.

Winnicott, D. W. (1988/1990). *Human Nature*. New York: Shocken Books.

Winnicott, D. W. (1992). *Psychoanalytic Explorations*. C. Winnicott, R. Shepherd, & M. Davis (Eds.). Cambridge, MA: Harvard University Press.

Zalman, S. (1973). *Likutei Amarim: Tanya*. Brooklyn, NY: Kehot Publication Society.

INDEX

Made in the USA
Middletown, DE
27 February 2021

34508667R00102